Lectio Divina

of the

Gospels

for the Liturgical Year

2021-2022

UNITED STATES CONFERENCE OF CATHOLIC BISHOPS

WASHINGTON, DC

Contents

March 27, 2022

April 3, 2022

April 10, 2022

April 17, 2022

April 24, 2022

May 1, 2022

May 8, 2022

May 15, 2022

May 22, 2022

May 26, 2022

May 29, 2022

June 5, 2022

June 12, 2022

Reading seeks for the sweetness of a blessed life,
meditation perceives it,
prayer asks for it,
contemplation tastes it.

Reading, as it were, puts food whole into the mouth,
meditation chews it and breaks it up,
prayer extracts its flavor,
contemplation is the sweetness itself
which gladdens and refreshes.

Reading works on the outside,
meditation on the pith,
prayer asks for what we long for,
contemplation gives us delight in the sweetness
which we have found.

—Guigo II, *The Ladder of Monks*, III (12th c.)

What Is *Lectio Divina* and How to Use This Book

Reading – Meditation – Prayer – Contemplation

Lectio divina or "divine reading" is a process of engaging with Christ, the Word of God. Through this sacred exercise, we enter into a closer relationship with the very Word himself, who communicates the love of the Father to us through the Holy Spirit.

Lectio divina has four steps in which we first hear what God has said (reading). We then take it in and reflect on it (meditation). From this our hearts are lifted up (prayer). Finally, after speaking to the Lord in prayer, we rest and listen for his message to us (contemplation).

This is the process of *lectio divina*. It is a conversation with God, grounded in God's own self-revelation to us. This helps us speak to God with a focus on what he has already told us about his relationship with humanity, his plans and desires for us, his promises, his admonitions, and his guidance on how we can live, so as to find true life in abundance in Christ.

Here is a brief description of each of the four steps:

Reading (*Lectio*)

Read the passage slowly and allow it to sink in.

If there is a passage that is particularly striking, and that you want to keep with you, consider committing it to memory, or writing it down to keep with you, so that you can re-read it throughout the day, and let it enter deeper into your spirit.

"Faith comes from what is heard, and what is heard comes through the word of Christ." (*Romans 10:17*)

"The word of God is living and effective, sharper than any two-edged sword, penetrating even between soul and spirit, joints and marrow, and able to discern reflections and thoughts of the heart." (*Hebrews 4:12*)

Meditation (*Meditatio*)

Read the passage again, and when something strikes you, a question arises in you, stop and meditate. Think about what God may be saying through it.

"It is the glory of God to conceal a matter,
*   and the glory of kings to fathom a matter."*
(*Proverbs 25:2*)

"I will ponder your precepts and consider your paths."
(*Psalm 119:15*)

Prayer (*Oratio*)

Speak to the Lord about what you have read and share what's on your mind and heart—offer and share with the Lord your thanksgiving, petition, concerns, doubts, or simply affirm, back to the Lord, the very word that he has spoken.

"Enter his gates with thanksgiving,
*   his courts with praise."*
(*Psalm 100:4*)

"Ask and it will be given to you; seek and you will find; knock and the door will be opened to you." (Matthew 7:7)

Contemplation (*Contemplatio*)

This is a quiet time, a time to rest in his presence and wait upon the Lord. It is a time where we allow the Lord to speak directly to our spirit from within us. It requires practice. But this allows us to be attentive to the Lord's voice, and by regular practice, our ability to hear God's voice will grow in daily life and daily situations, as we learn to focus our minds and hearts, our thoughts, our concerns, and our hopes toward him.

"My sheep hear my voice; I know them, and they follow me." (John 10:27)

"Be still and know that I am God!" (Psalm 46:11)

Applying This Process of *Lectio Divina* to the Liturgical Year

This *Lectio Divina of the Gospels for the Liturgical Year* book will take the reader through the Sundays and major feasts and solemnities of the liturgical year. It can be used for individual devotion and can also easily be used to assist in small group reflections in parishes and small faith groups. It offers a structured process for engaging with the Word of God. As the reader or group becomes more comfortable engaging with Scripture, this process can be more closely tailored to suit the path of growth that best fits the reader(s).

First, the *lectio divina* session is started by praying a prayer that is taken from a Mass collect from that liturgical week. Following that prayer, the main scripture passage for reflection is read, which is taken from the gospel reading for that day. This READING can be re-read, a few times, to let it sink in. Next, a set of three questions are offered to help in MEDITATION. These questions can also facilitate talking about the passage in a group setting. The individual then offers his or her personal PRAYER, responding to the Lord. In a group setting, people can speak out their prayers one at a time—this may help deepen the prayer response and further set the group's focus on the Lord.

Next, a structured set of passages and questions are offered that return the reader back to the gospel passage. This invites the reader to contemplate what the Lord is speaking and what it means for their life. It allows the individual or the prayer group to consider specific ways the Lord may be speaking into their life at that very moment. As each person begins to hear a response from the Lord—the Lord's word spoken directly and personally to them—that person can begin let that word flow through their life, by an interior change and a will to do what the Lord is asking of them. Through this step of CONTEMPLATION, we hear God's voice speaking to us, and it propels us to conversion of heart and mind.

After the closing prayer, time is given to choosing how to live out the fruit of your prayer. You know your heart and life best—if it's clear what God is asking of you, in faith, choose some way that you can put that request or teaching from the Lord into action that week. It could be a small act of faith that the Lord is asking, or perhaps, a more serious and important step that he is asking you to take. If there is nothing specific that comes to your mind, consider the question and suggestion offered in the *Living the Word This Week* section. This portion offers guidance on what concrete actions may be taken in our daily lives.

The *Lectio Divina of the Gospels for the Liturgical Year* offers a specific pattern of prayerful reading of God's Word. As you begin on this path, may the Lord's blessing follow you, and fall upon you, throughout the movement of seasons in this new liturgical year, and may your life, in turn, be a blessing upon others.

Lectio
Divina
of the
Gospels

November 28, 2021

Lectio Divina for the First Week of Advent

We begin our prayer:

In the name of the Father, and of the Son, and of the Holy Spirit. Amen.

Stir up your power, we pray, O Lord, and come,
that with you to protect us,
we may find rescue
from the pressing dangers of our sins,
and with you to set us free,
we may be found worthy of salvation.
Who live and reign with God the Father
in the unity of the Holy Spirit,
God, for ever and ever.

Collect, Friday of the First Week of Advent

Reading (*Lectio*)

Read the following Scripture two or three times.

Luke 21:25-28, 34-36

> Jesus said to his disciples: "There will be signs in the sun, the moon, and the stars, and on earth nations will be in dismay, perplexed by the roaring of the sea and the waves. People will die of fright in anticipation of what is coming upon the world, for the powers of the heavens will be shaken. And then they will see the Son of Man coming in a cloud with power and great glory. But when these signs begin to happen, stand erect and raise your heads because your redemption is at hand.

> "Beware that your hearts do not become drowsy from carousing and drunkenness and the anxieties of daily life, and that day catch you by surprise like a trap. For that day will assault everyone who lives on the face of the earth. Be vigilant at all times and pray that you have the strength to escape the tribulations that are imminent and to stand before the Son of Man."

Meditation (*Meditatio*)

After the reading, take some time to reflect in silence on one or more of the following questions:

- What word or words in this passage caught your attention?
- What in this passage comforted you?
- What in this passage challenged you?

If practicing lectio divina as a family or in a group, after the reflection time, invite the participants to share their responses.

Prayer (*Oratio*)

Read the scripture passage one more time. Bring to the Lord the praise, petition, or thanksgiving that the Word inspires in you.

Contemplation (*Contemplatio*)

Read the Scripture again, followed by this reflection:

∾ What conversion of mind, heart, and life is the Lord asking of me?

_____

_____

_____

_____

∾ *There will be signs in the sun, the moon, and the stars.* How do I experience God's presence and majesty in the natural world? How can I become more aware of God's gift of creation?

_____

_____

_____

_____

≈ *Then they will see the Son of Man coming in a cloud with power and great glory.* When have I been most aware of God's power acting in my life? How do my actions give glory to God?

_____

_____

_____

_____

≈ *Stand erect and raise your heads because your redemption is at hand.* How can I grow in my longing for salvation? In this Advent, how can I prepare my heart for Christ's coming?

_____

_____

_____

_____

≈ *After a period of silent reflection and/or discussion, all recite the Lord's Prayer and the following:*

Closing Prayer

Your ways, O LORD, make known to me;
   teach me your paths,
Guide me in your truth and teach me,
   for you are God my savior,
   and for you I wait all the day.

Good and upright is the LORD;
   thus he shows sinners the way.
He guides the humble to justice,
   and teaches the humble his way.

All the paths of the LORD are kindness and constancy
   toward those who keep his covenant and his decrees.
The friendship of the LORD is with those who fear him,
   and his covenant, for their instruction.

From Psalm 25

Living the Word This Week

How can I make my life a gift for others in charity?

Before going to sleep each night this week, reflect on your day to become more attentive to God working in your life.

December 5, 2021

Lectio Divina for the Second Week of Advent

We begin our prayer:

In the name of the Father, and of the Son, and of the Holy Spirit. Amen.

O God, who have shown forth your salvation
to all the ends of the earth,
grant, we pray,
that we may look forward in joy
to the glorious Nativity of Christ.
Who lives and reigns with you in the unity of the Holy Spirit,
God, for ever and ever.

Collect, Tuesday of the Second Week of Advent

Reading (*Lectio*)

Read the following Scripture two or three times.

Luke 3:1-6

In the fifteenth year of the reign of Tiberius Caesar, when Pontius Pilate was governor of Judea, and Herod was tetrarch of Galilee, and his brother Philip tetrarch of the region of Ituraea and Trachonitis, and Lysanias was tetrarch of Abilene, during the high priesthood of Annas and Caiaphas, the word of God came to John the son of Zechariah in the desert. John went throughout the whole region of the Jordan, proclaiming a baptism of repentance for the forgiveness of sins, as it is written in the book of the words of the prophet Isaiah:

A voice of one crying out in the desert:
"Prepare the way of the Lord,
    make straight his paths.
Every valley shall be filled
    and every mountain and hill shall be made low.
The winding roads shall be made straight,
    and the rough ways made smooth,
and all flesh shall see the salvation of God."

Meditation (*Meditatio*)

After the reading, take some time to reflect in silence on one or more of the following questions:

- What word or words in this passage caught your attention?
- What in this passage comforted you?
- What in this passage challenged you?

If practicing lectio divina as a family or in a group, after the reflection time, invite the participants to share their responses.

Prayer (*Oratio*)

Read the scripture passage one more time. Bring to the Lord the praise, petition, or thanksgiving that the Word inspires in you.

Contemplation (*Contemplatio*)

Read the Scripture again, followed by this reflection:

∿ What conversion of mind, heart, and life is the Lord asking of me?

_____

_____

_____

_____

∿ *John went throughout the whole region of the Jordan.* Where is God calling me to go? To what regions of my neighborhood, parish, workplace can I bring compassion and loving service?

_____

_____

_____

_____

∾ *A voice of one crying out in the desert.* When have I felt like a voice crying out in the desert? When have I failed to use my voice when I should have?

_____

_____

_____

_____

∾ *All flesh shall see the salvation of God.* How can I be more open to encountering Jesus? Whom can I help to encounter Jesus?

_____

_____

_____

_____

∾ *After a period of silent reflection and/or discussion, all recite the Lord's Prayer and the following:*

Closing Prayer

When the LORD brought back the captives of Zion,
　　we were like men dreaming.
Then our mouth was filled with laughter,
　　and our tongue with rejoicing.

Then they said among the nations,
  "The LORD has done great things for them."
The LORD has done great things for us;
  we are glad indeed.

Restore our fortunes, O LORD,
  like the torrents in the southern desert.
Those who sow in tears
  shall reap rejoicing.

Although they go forth weeping,
  carrying the seed to be sown,
They shall come back rejoicing,
  carrying their sheaves.

From Psalm 126

Living the Word This Week

How can I make my life a gift for others in charity?

Invite someone to join you at Mass or at a parish Advent class or prayer service.

December 8, 2021

Lectio Divina for the Solemnity of the Immaculate Conception

We begin our prayer:

In the name of the Father, and of the Son, and of the Holy Spirit. Amen.

O God, who by the Immaculate Conception of the Blessed Virgin
prepared a worthy dwelling for your Son,
grant, we pray,
that, as you preserved her from every stain
by virtue of the Death of your Son, which you foresaw,
so, through her intercession,
we, too, may be cleansed and admitted to your presence.
Through our Lord Jesus Christ, your Son,
who lives and reigns with you in the unity of the Holy Spirit,
God, for ever and ever.

Collect, Solemnity of the Immaculate Conception

Reading (*Lectio*)

Read the following Scripture two or three times.

Luke 1:26-38

The angel Gabriel was sent from God to a town of Galilee called Nazareth, to a virgin betrothed to a man named Joseph, of the house of David, and the virgin's name was Mary. And coming to her, he said, "Hail, full of grace! The Lord is with you." But she was greatly troubled at what was said and pondered what sort of greeting this might be. Then the angel said to her, "Do not be afraid, Mary, for you have found favor with God. Behold, you will conceive in your womb and bear a son, and you shall name him Jesus. He will be great and will be called Son of the Most High, and the Lord God will give him the throne of David his father, and he will rule over the house of Jacob forever, and of his Kingdom there will be no end." But Mary said to the angel, "How can this be, since I have no relations with a man?" And the angel said to her in reply, "The Holy Spirit will come upon you, and the power of the Most High will overshadow you. Therefore the child to be born will be called holy, the Son of God. And behold, Elizabeth, your relative, has also conceived a son in her old age, and this is the sixth month for her who was called barren; for nothing will be impossible for God." Mary said, "Behold, I am the handmaid of the Lord. May it be done to me according to your word." Then the angel departed from her.

Meditation (*Meditatio*)

After the reading, take some time to reflect in silence on one or more of the following questions:

- What word or words in this passage caught your attention?
- What in this passage comforted you?
- What in this passage challenged you?

If practicing lectio divina as a family or in a group, after the reflection time, invite the participants to share their responses.

Prayer (*Oratio*)

Read the scripture passage one more time. Bring to the Lord the praise, petition, or thanksgiving that the Word inspires in you.

Contemplation (*Contemplatio*)

Read the Scripture again, followed by this reflection:

∿ What conversion of mind, heart, and life is the Lord asking of me?

_____

_____

_____

_____

~ *For you have found favor with God.* When have I felt the favor of God in my life? How can I recognize God's presence and favor in those I meet?

_____

_____

_____

_____

~ *The power of the Most High will overshadow you.* How have I experienced God's power in my life? What is my response to God's power and majesty?

_____

_____

_____

_____

~ *This is the sixth month for her who was called barren.* When has my prayer life felt barren and dry? What lifestyle changes can I make to prioritize my relationship with God?

_____

_____

_____

_____

~ After a period of silent reflection and/or discussion, all recite the Lord's Prayer and the following:

Closing Prayer

Sing to the LORD a new song,
    for he has done wondrous deeds;
His right hand has won victory for him,
    his holy arm.

The LORD has made his salvation known:
    in the sight of the nations he has revealed his justice.
He has remembered his kindness and his faithfulness
    toward the house of Israel.

All the ends of the earth have seen
    the salvation by our God.
Sing joyfully to the LORD, all you lands;
    break into song; sing praise.

From Psalm 98

Living the Word This Week

How can I make my life a gift for others in charity?

Pray a Rosary for the intentions of those who have nurtured your faith.

December 12, 2021

Lectio Divina for the Third Week of Advent

We begin our prayer:

In the name of the Father, and of the Son, and of the Holy Spirit. Amen.

Grant, we pray, almighty God,
that the coming solemnity of your Son
may bestow healing upon us in this present life
and bring us the rewards of life eternal.
Through our Lord Jesus Christ, your Son,
who lives and reigns with you in the unity of the Holy Spirit,
God, for ever and ever.

Collect, Wednesday of the Third Week of Advent

Reading (*Lectio*)

Read the following Scripture two or three times.

Luke 3:10-18

The crowds asked John the Baptist, "What should we do?" He
said to them in reply, "Whoever has two cloaks should share with

the person who has none. And whoever has food should do likewise." Even tax collectors came to be baptized and they said to him, "Teacher, what should we do?" He answered them, "Stop collecting more than what is prescribed." Soldiers also asked him, "And what is it that we should do?" He told them, "Do not practice extortion, do not falsely accuse anyone, and be satisfied with your wages."

Now the people were filled with expectation, and all were asking in their hearts whether John might be the Christ. John answered them all, saying, "I am baptizing you with water, but one mightier than I is coming. I am not worthy to loosen the thongs of his sandals. He will baptize you with the Holy Spirit and fire. His winnowing fan is in his hand to clear his threshing floor and to gather the wheat into his barn, but the chaff he will burn with unquenchable fire." Exhorting them in many other ways, he preached good news to the people.

Meditation (*Meditatio*)

After the reading, take some time to reflect in silence on one or more of the following questions:

- What word or words in this passage caught your attention?
- What in this passage comforted you?
- What in this passage challenged you?

If practicing lectio divina as a family or in a group, after the reflection time, invite the participants to share their responses.

Prayer (*Oratio*)

Read the scripture passage one more time. Bring to the Lord the praise, petition, or thanksgiving that the Word inspires in you.

Contemplation (*Contemplatio*)

Read the Scripture again, followed by this reflection:

≈ What conversion of mind, heart, and life is the Lord asking of me?

_____

_____

_____

_____

≈ *Do not practice extortion, do not falsely accuse anyone, and be satisfied with your wages.* How can I be kinder and more honest in my speech? How do envy and greed disrupt my relationship with material goods?

_____

_____

_____

_____

∾ *Now the people were filled with expectation.* For what do I hope? How does my faith in God fulfill my longings?

_____

_____

_____

_____

∾ *His winnowing fan is in his hand to clear his threshing floor and to gather the wheat into his barn.* What sinful parts of my life need to be winnowed away? What spiritual gifts do I treasure the most?

_____

_____

_____

_____

∾ *After a period of silent reflection and/or discussion, all recite the Lord's Prayer and the following:*

Closing Prayer

God indeed is my savior;
    I am confident and unafraid.
My strength and my courage is the LORD,
    and he has been my savior.
With joy you will draw water
      at the fountain of salvation.

Give thanks to the LORD, acclaim his name;
      among the nations make known his deeds,
      proclaim how exalted is his name.

Sing praise to the LORD for his glorious achievement;
      let this be known throughout all the earth.
Shout with exultation, O city of Zion,
      for great in your midst
        is the Holy One of Israel!

From Isaiah 12

Living the Word This Week

How can I make my life a gift for others in charity?

Make a good examination of conscience and plan to receive the
Sacrament of Penance before Christmas.

December 19, 2021

Lectio Divina for the Fourth Week of Advent

We begin our prayer:

In the name of the Father, and of the Son, and of the Holy Spirit. Amen.

Almighty ever-living God,
as we see how the Nativity of your Son
according to the flesh draws near,
we pray that to us, your unworthy servants,
mercy may flow from your Word,
who chose to become flesh of the Virgin Mary
and establish among us his dwelling,
Jesus Christ our Lord.
Who lives and reigns with you in the unity of the Holy Spirit,
God, for ever and ever.

Collect, December 23

Reading (*Lectio*)

Read the following Scripture two or three times.

Luke 1:39-45

> Mary set out and traveled to the hill country in haste to a town of
> Judah, where she entered the house of Zechariah and greeted Eliz-
> abeth. When Elizabeth heard Mary's greeting, the infant leaped in
> her womb, and Elizabeth, filled with the Holy Spirit, cried out in a
> loud voice and said, "Blessed are you among women, and blessed
> is the fruit of your womb. And how does this happen to me, that
> the mother of my Lord should come to me? For at the moment the
> sound of your greeting reached my ears, the infant in my womb
> leaped for joy. Blessed are you who believed that what was spoken
> to you by the Lord would be fulfilled."

Meditation (*Meditatio*)

*After the reading, take some time to reflect in silence on one or more of the
following questions:*

- What word or words in this passage caught your attention?
- What in this passage comforted you?
- What in this passage challenged you?

*If practicing lectio divina as a family or in a group, after the reflection time,
invite the participants to share their responses.*

Prayer (*Oratio*)

Read the scripture passage one more time. Bring to the Lord the praise, petition, or thanksgiving that the Word inspires in you.

Contemplation (*Contemplatio*)

Read the Scripture again, followed by this reflection:

≈ What conversion of mind, heart, and life is the Lord asking of me?

_____

_____

_____

_____

≈ *Mary set out and traveled to the hill country in haste to a town of Judah.* When have I approached God in haste? When do I come in haste to the aid of my brothers and sisters?

_____

_____

_____

_____

≈ *When Elizabeth heard Mary's greeting, the infant leaped in her womb.* How have I heard God speaking to me? How have I responded to God's voice?

_____

_____

_____

_____

≈ *Blessed are you among women, and blessed is the fruit of your womb.* For what blessings am I most thankful? How have God's blessings borne fruit in my life?

_____

_____

_____

_____

≈ *After a period of silent reflection and/or discussion, all recite the Lord's Prayer and the following:*

Closing Prayer

O shepherd of Israel, hearken,
> from your throne upon the cherubim, shine forth.
Rouse your power,
> and come to save us.

Once again, O Lord of hosts,
    look down from heaven, and see;
take care of this vine,
    and protect what your right hand has planted
    the son of man whom you yourself made strong.

May your help be with the man of your right hand,
    with the son of man whom you yourself made strong.
Then we will no more withdraw from you;
    give us new life, and we will call upon your name.

From Psalm 80

Living the Word This Week

How can I make my life a gift for others in charity?

Research your parish or diocesan pro-life activities and prayerfully discern how you might become involved.

December 25, 2021

Lectio Divina for the Solemnity of Christmas

We begin our prayer:

In the name of the Father, and of the Son, and of the Holy Spirit. Amen.

Grant, we pray, almighty God,
that, as we are bathed in the new radiance of your incarnate Word,
the light of faith, which illumines our minds,
may also shine through in our deeds.
Through our Lord Jesus Christ, your Son,
who lives and reigns with you in the unity of the Holy Spirit,
God, for ever and ever.

Collect, Christmas, Mass at Dawn

Reading (*Lectio*)

Read the following Scripture two or three times.

Luke 2:1-14

In those days a decree went out from Caesar Augustus that the whole world should be enrolled. This was the first enrollment, when Quirinius was governor of Syria. So all went to be enrolled, each to his own town. And Joseph too went up from Galilee from the town of Nazareth to Judea, to the city of David that is called Bethlehem, because he was of the house and family of David, to be enrolled with Mary, his betrothed, who was with child. While they were there, the time came for her to have her child, and she gave birth to her firstborn son. She wrapped him in swaddling clothes and laid him in a manger, because there was no room for them in the inn.

Now there were shepherds in that region living in the fields and keeping the night watch over their flock. The angel of the Lord appeared to them and the glory of the Lord shone around them, and they were struck with great fear. The angel said to them, "Do not be afraid; for behold, I proclaim to you good news of great joy that will be for all the people. For today in the city of David a savior has been born for you who is Christ and Lord. And this will be a sign for you: you will find an infant wrapped in swaddling clothes and lying in a manger." And suddenly there was a multitude of the heavenly host with the angel, praising God and saying:

"Glory to God in the highest
    and on earth peace to those on whom his favor rests."

Meditation (*Meditatio*)

After the reading, take some time to reflect in silence on one or more of the following questions:

- What word or words in this passage caught your attention?
- What in this passage comforted you?
- What in this passage challenged you?

If practicing lectio divina as a family or in a group, after the reflection time, invite the participants to share their responses.

Prayer (*Oratio*)

Read the scripture passage one more time. Bring to the Lord the praise, petition, or thanksgiving that the Word inspires in you.

Contemplation (*Contemplatio*)

Read the Scripture again, followed by this reflection:

∼ What conversion of mind, heart, and life is the Lord asking of me?

———————————————————————————

———————————————————————————

———————————————————————————

———————————————————————————

∼ *There was no room for them in the inn.* For whom do I need to make room in my life and heart? How can I be more welcoming to those I meet?

_____

_____

_____

_____

∼ *Do not be afraid; for behold, I proclaim to you good news of great joy that will be for all the people.* What fears and worries keep me from proclaiming the Gospel? How can I be more diligent about sharing my faith?

_____

_____

_____

_____

∼ *Glory to God in the highest/ and on earth peace to those on whom his favor rests.* How does my life bring glory to God? How can I be a messenger of God's peace?

_____

_____

_____

_____

~ *After a period of silent reflection and/or discussion, all recite the Lord's Prayer and the following:*

Closing Prayer

Sing to the LORD a new song;
    sing to the LORD, all you lands.
Sing to the LORD; bless his name.

Announce his salvation, day after day.
Tell his glory among the nations;
    among all peoples, his wondrous deeds.

Let the heavens be glad and the earth rejoice;
    let the sea and what fills it resound;
    let the plains be joyful and all that is in them!
Then shall all the trees of the forest exult.

They shall exult before the LORD, for he comes;
    for he comes to rule the earth.
He shall rule the world with justice
    and the peoples with his constancy.

From Psalm 96

Living the Word This Week

How can I make my life a gift for others in charity?

Read *Disciples Called to Witness* (*www.usccb.org/beliefs-and-teachings/how-we-teach/new-evangelization/disciples-called-to-witness*) and reflect on ways that you can implement its suggestions.

December 26, 2021

Lectio Divina for the Feast of the Holy Family

We begin our prayer:

In the name of the Father, and of the Son, and of the Holy Spirit. Amen.

O God, who were pleased to give us
the shining example of the Holy Family,
graciously grant that we may imitate them
in practicing the virtues of family life and in the bonds of charity,
and so, in the joy of your house,
delight one day in eternal rewards.
Through our Lord Jesus Christ, your Son,
who lives and reigns with you in the unity of the Holy Spirit,
God, for ever and ever.

Collect, Feast of the Holy Family

Reading (*Lectio*)

Read the following Scripture two or three times.

Luke 2:41-52

Each year Jesus' parents went to Jerusalem for the feast of Passover, and when he was twelve years old, they went up according to festival custom. After they had completed its days, as they were returning, the boy Jesus remained behind in Jerusalem, but his parents did not know it. Thinking that he was in the caravan, they journeyed for a day and looked for him among their relatives and acquaintances, but not finding him, they returned to Jerusalem to look for him. After three days they found him in the temple, sitting in the midst of the teachers, listening to them and asking them questions, and all who heard him were astounded at his understanding and his answers. When his parents saw him, they were astonished, and his mother said to him, "Son, why have you done this to us? Your father and I have been looking for you with great anxiety." And he said to them, "Why were you looking for me? Did you not know that I must be in my Father's house?" But they did not understand what he said to them. He went down with them and came to Nazareth, and was obedient to them; and his mother kept all these things in her heart. And Jesus advanced in wisdom and age and favor before God and man.

Meditation (*Meditatio*)

After the reading, take some time to reflect in silence on one or more of the following questions:

- What word or words in this passage caught your attention?
- What in this passage comforted you?
- What in this passage challenged you?

If practicing lectio divina as a family or in a group, after the reflection time, invite the participants to share their responses.

Prayer (*Oratio*)

Read the scripture passage one more time. Bring to the Lord the praise, petition, or thanksgiving that the Word inspires in you.

Contemplation (*Contemplatio*)

Read the Scripture again, followed by this reflection:

∼ What conversion of mind, heart, and life is the Lord asking of me?

_____

_____

_____

_____

∼ *All who heard him were astounded at his understanding and his answers.* What sources do I use to learn about my faith? What spiritual guides have enriched my understanding?

_____

_____

_____

_____

∼ *But they did not understand what he said to them.* When have I fallen short in my understanding of faith? How can I remedy these shortcomings?

_____

_____

_____

_____

∼ *And Jesus advanced in wisdom and age and favor before God and man.* How can I grow in wisdom? How have I experienced God's favor?

_____

_____

_____

_____

~ After a period of silent reflection and/or discussion, all recite the Lord's Prayer and the following:

Closing Prayer

How lovely is your dwelling place, O LORD of hosts!
   My soul yearns and pines for the courts of the LORD.
My heart and my flesh cry out for the living God.

Happy they who dwell in your house!
   Continually they praise you.
Happy the men whose strength you are!
   Their hearts are set upon the pilgrimage.

O LORD of hosts, hear our prayer;
   hearken, O God of Jacob!
O God, behold our shield,
   and look upon the face of your anointed.

From Psalm 84

Living the Word This Week

How can I make my life a gift for others in charity?

Make a plan for growing in the knowledge and practice of your faith in the new year, through reading, classes, and apostolic action.

January 1, 2022

Lectio Divina for the Solemnity of Mary, Mother of God

We begin our prayer:

In the name of the Father, and of the Son, and of the Holy Spirit. Amen.

Almighty ever-living God,
splendor of faithful souls,
graciously be pleased to fill the world with your glory,
and show yourself to all peoples by the radiance of your light.
Through our Lord Jesus Christ, your Son,
who lives and reigns with you in the unity of the Holy Spirit,
God, for ever and ever.

Collect, Second Sunday after the Nativity

Reading (*Lectio*)

Read the following Scripture two or three times.

Luke 2:16-21

The shepherds went in haste to Bethlehem and found Mary and Joseph, and the infant lying in the manger. When they saw this, they made known the message that had been told them about this child. All who heard it were amazed by what had been told them by the shepherds. And Mary kept all these things, reflecting on them in her heart. Then the shepherds returned, glorifying and praising God for all they had heard and seen, just as it had been told to them.

When eight days were completed for his circumcision, he was named Jesus, the name given him by the angel before he was conceived in the womb.

Meditation (*Meditatio*)

After the reading, take some time to reflect in silence on one or more of the following questions:

- What word or words in this passage caught your attention?
- What in this passage comforted you?
- What in this passage challenged you?

If practicing lectio divina as a family or in a group, after the reflection time, invite the participants to share their responses.

Prayer (*Oratio*)

Read the scripture passage one more time. Bring to the Lord the praise, petition, or thanksgiving that the Word inspires in you.

Contemplation (*Contemplatio*)

Read the Scripture again, followed by this reflection:

∾ What conversion of mind, heart, and life is the Lord asking of me?

_____

_____

_____

_____

∾ *The shepherds . . . found Mary and Joseph, and the infant lying in the manger.* Where do I find God? How can I be more attentive to God's presence?

_____

_____

_____

_____

~ *Then the shepherds returned, glorifying and praising God for all they had heard and seen.* For what shall I praise God this week? How can I help others encounter God's glory?

_____

_____

_____

_____

~ *Just as it had been told to them.* When has God fulfilled his promise to me? How do I grow in my trust for God and his promises?

_____

_____

_____

_____

~ *After a period of silent reflection and/or discussion, all recite the Lord's Prayer and the following:*

Closing Prayer

May God have pity on us and bless us;
   may he let his face shine upon us.
So may your way be known upon earth;
   among all nations, your salvation.

May the nations be glad and exult
    because you rule the peoples in equity;
    the nations on the earth you guide.

May the peoples praise you, O God;
    may all the peoples praise you!
May God bless us,
    and may all the ends of the earth fear him

From Psalm 67

Living the Word This Week

How can I make my life a gift for others in charity?

In the new year, resolve to pray before Jesus present in the Blessed
Sacrament at least monthly.

January 2, 2022

Lectio Divina for the Solemnity of the Epiphany

We begin our prayer:

In the name of the Father, and of the Son, and of the Holy Spirit. Amen.

May the splendor of your majesty, O Lord, we pray,
shed its light upon our hearts,
that we may pass through the shadows of this world
and reach the brightness of our eternal home.
Through our Lord Jesus Christ, your Son,
who lives and reigns with you in the unity of the Holy Spirit,
God, for ever and ever.

Collect, Solemnity of the Epiphany, Vigil Mass

Reading (*Lectio*)

Read the following Scripture two or three times.

Matthew 2:1-12

When Jesus was born in Bethlehem of Judea, in the days of King Herod, behold, magi from the east arrived in Jerusalem, saying, "Where is the newborn king of the Jews? We saw his star at its rising and have come to do him homage." When King Herod heard this, he was greatly troubled, and all Jerusalem with him. Assembling all the chief priests and the scribes of the people, he inquired of them where the Christ was to be born. They said to him, "In Bethlehem of Judea, for thus it has been written through the prophet:

And you, Bethlehem, land of Judah,
*   are by no means least among the rulers of Judah;*
since from you shall come a ruler,
*   who is to shepherd my people Israel."*

Then Herod called the magi secretly and ascertained from them the time of the star's appearance. He sent them to Bethlehem and said, "Go and search diligently for the child. When you have found him, bring me word, that I too may go and do him homage." After their audience with the king they set out. And behold, the star that they had seen at its rising preceded them, until it came and stopped over the place where the child was. They were overjoyed at seeing the star, and on entering the house they saw the child with Mary his mother. They prostrated themselves and did him homage. Then they opened their treasures and offered him gifts of gold, frankincense, and myrrh. And having been warned in a dream not to return to Herod, they departed for their country by another way.

Meditation (*Meditatio*)

After the reading, take some time to reflect in silence on one or more of the following questions:

- What word or words in this passage caught your attention?
- What in this passage comforted you?
- What in this passage challenged you?

If practicing lectio divina as a family or in a group, after the reflection time, invite the participants to share their responses.

Prayer (*Oratio*)

Read the scripture passage one more time. Bring to the Lord the praise, petition, or thanksgiving that the Word inspires in you.

Contemplation (*Contemplatio*)

Read the Scripture again, followed by this reflection:

≈ What conversion of mind, heart, and life is the Lord asking of me?

_____

_____

_____

_____

~ *When King Herod heard this, he was greatly troubled, and all Jerusalem with him.* What events or circumstances cause anxiety for me? How can I be a person who brings peace to my community?

_____

_____

_____

_____

~ *Go and search diligently for the child.* For what am I searching? How can I be more diligent in my efforts to grow in holiness?

_____

_____

_____

_____

~ *They prostrated themselves and did him homage.* How do I show honor and reverence for God? How can I grow in humility?

_____

_____

_____

_____

≈ After a period of silent reflection and/or discussion, all recite the Lord's Prayer and the following:

Closing Prayer

O God, with your judgment endow the king,
    and with your justice, the king's son;
He shall govern your people with justice
    and your afflicted ones with judgment.

Justice shall flower in his days,
    and profound peace, till the moon be no more.
May he rule from sea to sea,
    and from the River to the ends of the earth.

The kings of Tarshish and the Isles shall offer gifts;
    the kings of Arabia and Seba shall bring tribute.
All kings shall pay him homage,
    all nations shall serve him.

For he shall rescue the poor when he cries out,
    and the afflicted when he has no one to help him.
He shall have pity for the lowly and the poor;
    the lives of the poor he shall save.

From Psalm 72

Living the Word This Week

How can I make my life a gift for others in charity?

When attending Mass this week, make a special effort to be attentive to the prayers and actions of the Eucharistic liturgy and to receive the Eucharist with reverence.

January 9, 2022

Lectio Divina for the Feast of the Baptism of the Lord

We begin our prayer:

In the name of the Father, and of the Son, and of the Holy Spirit. Amen.

Almighty ever-living God,
who, when Christ had been baptized in the River Jordan
and as the Holy Spirit descended upon him,
solemnly declared him your beloved Son,
grant that your children by adoption,
reborn of water and the Holy Spirit,
may always be well pleasing to you.
Through our Lord Jesus Christ, your Son,
who lives and reigns with you in the unity of the Holy Spirit,
God, for ever and ever.

Collect, Baptism of the Lord

Reading (*Lectio*)

Read the following Scripture two or three times.

Luke 3:15-16, 21-22

The people were filled with expectation, and all were asking in their hearts whether John might be the Christ. John answered them all, saying, "I am baptizing you with water, but one mightier than I is coming. I am not worthy to loosen the thongs of his sandals. He will baptize you with the Holy Spirit and fire."

After all the people had been baptized and Jesus also had been baptized and was praying, heaven was opened and the Holy Spirit descended upon him in bodily form like a dove. And a voice came from heaven, "You are my beloved Son; with you I am well pleased."

Meditation (*Meditatio*)

After the reading, take some time to reflect in silence on one or more of the following questions:

- What word or words in this passage caught your attention?
- What in this passage comforted you?
- What in this passage challenged you?

If practicing lectio divina as a family or in a group, after the reflection time, invite the participants to share their responses.

Prayer (*Oratio*)

Read the scripture passage one more time. Bring to the Lord the praise, petition, or thanksgiving that the Word inspires in you.

Contemplation (*Contemplatio*)

Read the Scripture again, followed by this reflection:

≈ What conversion of mind, heart, and life is the Lord asking of me?

_____

_____

_____

_____

≈ *I am not worthy to loosen the thongs of his sandals.* How can I serve God more faithfully? How can I serve my brothers and sisters in need?

_____

_____

_____

_____

~ *He will baptize you with the Holy Spirit and fire.* How does my faith inspire my actions? How are the gifts and fruits of the Spirit present in my life?

_____

_____

_____

_____

~ *You are my beloved Son; with you I am well pleased.* How can I grow in my love of Jesus? How can I see Jesus in everyone I encounter?

_____

_____

_____

_____

~ *After a period of silent reflection and/or discussion, all recite the Lord's Prayer and the following:*

Closing Prayer

O Lord, my God, you are great indeed!
    you are clothed with majesty and glory,
robed in light as with a cloak.
    You have spread out the heavens like a tent-cloth;

You have constructed your palace upon the waters.
   You make the clouds your chariot;
you travel on the wings of the wind.
   You make the winds your messengers,
and flaming fire your ministers.

How manifold are your works, O Lord!
   In wisdom you have wrought them all—
the earth is full of your creatures;
   the sea also, great and wide,
in which are schools without number
   of living things both small and great.

They look to you to give them food in due time.
   When you give it to them, they gather it;
when you open your hand, they are filled with good things.

If you take away their breath, they perish and return to the dust.
   When you send forth your spirit, they are created,
and you renew the face of the earth.

From Psalm 104

Living the Word This Week

How can I make my life a gift for others in charity?

Research volunteer opportunities in your parish and find ways to share your gifts with your parish community.

January 16, 2022

Lectio Divina for the Second Week in Ordinary Time

We begin our prayer:

In the name of the Father, and of the Son, and of the Holy Spirit. Amen.

Almighty ever-living God,
who govern all things,
both in heaven and on earth,
mercifully hear the pleading of your people
and bestow your peace on our times.
Through our Lord Jesus Christ, your Son,
who lives and reigns with you in the unity of the Holy Spirit,
God, for ever and ever.

Collect, Second Sunday in Ordinary Time

Reading (*Lectio*)

Read the following Scripture two or three times.

John 2:1-11

> There was a wedding at Cana in Galilee, and the mother of Jesus was there. Jesus and his disciples were also invited to the wedding. When the wine ran short, the mother of Jesus said to him, "They have no wine." And Jesus said to her, "Woman, how does your concern affect me? My hour has not yet come." His mother said to the servers, "Do whatever he tells you." Now there were six stone water jars there for Jewish ceremonial washings, each holding twenty to thirty gallons. Jesus told the them, "Fill the jars with water." So they filled them to the brim. Then he told them, "Draw some out now and take it to the headwaiter." So they took it. And when the headwaiter tasted the water that had become wine, without knowing where it came from—although the servers who had drawn the water knew—, the headwaiter called the bridegroom and said to him, "Everyone serves good wine first, and then when people have drunk freely, an inferior one; but you have kept the good wine until now." Jesus did this as the beginning of his signs at Cana in Galilee and so revealed his glory, and his disciples began to believe in him.

Meditation (*Meditatio*)

After the reading, take some time to reflect in silence on one or more of the following questions:

- What word or words in this passage caught your attention?
- What in this passage comforted you?
- What in this passage challenged you?

If practicing lectio divina as a family or in a group, after the reflection time, invite the participants to share their responses.

Prayer (*Oratio*)

Read the scripture passage one more time. Bring to the Lord the praise, petition, or thanksgiving that the Word inspires in you.

Contemplation (*Contemplatio*)

Read the Scripture again, followed by this reflection:

∼ What conversion of mind, heart, and life is the Lord asking of me?

_____

_____

_____

_____

∼ When the wine ran short, the mother of Jesus said to him, "They have no wine." For what do I need to ask God? How can I be more attentive to the needs of others?

_____

_____

_____

_____

~ *The headwaiter tasted the water that had become wine, without knowing where it came from.* When has God's goodness surprised me? How can I become more grateful for God's loving kindness?

_____

_____

_____

_____

~ *You have kept the good wine until now.* When do I hold on to the gifts God gives me instead of sharing them? How can I be more generous?

_____

_____

_____

_____

~ *After a period of silent reflection and/or discussion, all recite the Lord's Prayer and the following:*

Closing Prayer

Sing to the LORD a new song;
    sing to the LORD, all you lands.
Sing to the LORD; bless his name.

Announce his salvation, day after day.
Tell his glory among the nations;
    among all peoples, his wondrous deeds.

Give to the LORD, you families of nations,
    give to the LORD glory and praise;
    give to the LORD the glory due his name!

Worship the LORD in holy attire.
    Tremble before him, all the earth;
Say among the nations: The LORD is king.
    He governs the peoples with equity.

From Psalm 96

Living the Word This Week

How can I make my life a gift for others in charity?

Share your gifts by making a contribution to a parish food pantry, to the Saint Vincent de Paul Society, or to Catholic Charities.

January 23, 2022

Lectio Divina for the Third Week in Ordinary Time

We begin our prayer:

In the name of the Father, and of the Son, and of the Holy Spirit. Amen.

Almighty ever-living God,
direct our actions according to your good pleasure,
that in the name of your beloved Son
we may abound in good works.
Through our Lord Jesus Christ, your Son,
who lives and reigns with you in the unity of the Holy Spirit,
God, for ever and ever.

Collect, Third Sunday in Ordinary Time

Reading (*Lectio*)

Read the following Scripture two or three times.

Luke 1:1-4; 4:14-21

Since many have undertaken to compile a narrative of the events that have been fulfilled among us, just as those who were eyewitnesses from the beginning and ministers of the word have handed them down to us, I too have decided, after investigating everything accurately anew, to write it down in an orderly sequence for you, most excellent Theophilus, so that you may realize the certainty of the teachings you have received.

Jesus returned to Galilee in the power of the Spirit, and news of him spread throughout the whole region. He taught in their synagogues and was praised by all.

He came to Nazareth, where he had grown up, and went according to his custom into the synagogue on the sabbath day. He stood up to read and was handed a scroll of the prophet Isaiah. He unrolled the scroll and found the passage where it was written:

The Spirit of the Lord is upon me,
because he has anointed me
to bring glad tidings to the poor.
He has sent me to proclaim liberty to captives
and recovery of sight to the blind,
to let the oppressed go free,
and to proclaim a year acceptable to the Lord.

Rolling up the scroll, he handed it back to the attendant and sat down, and the eyes of all in the synagogue looked intently at him. He said to them, "Today this Scripture passage is fulfilled in your hearing."

Meditation (*Meditatio*)

After the reading, take some time to reflect in silence on one or more of the following questions:

- What word or words in this passage caught your attention?
- What in this passage comforted you?
- What in this passage challenged you?

If practicing lectio divina as a family or in a group, after the reflection time, invite the participants to share their responses.

Prayer (*Oratio*)

Read the scripture passage one more time. Bring to the Lord the praise, petition, or thanksgiving that the Word inspires in you.

Contemplation (*Contemplatio*)

Read the Scripture again, followed by this reflection:

� What conversion of mind, heart, and life is the Lord asking of me?

〜 *Many have undertaken to compile a narrative of the events that have been fulfilled among us.* Who has been most influential in helping you understand the faith? How can you share your faith story with others?

_____

_____

_____

_____

〜 *So that you may realize the certainty of the teachings you have received.* When have I experienced doubt about Church teaching? What authoritative sources can help me learn more about what the Church teaches?

_____

_____

_____

_____

〜 *He has sent me to proclaim liberty to captives / and recovery of sight to the blind, / to let the oppressed go free.* From what sinful behaviors do I need God's grace to free me? How can I help to free others from the chains of oppression, prejudice, and loneliness?

_____

_____

_____

_____

~ *After a period of silent reflection and/or discussion, all recite the Lord's Prayer and the following:*

Closing Prayer

The law of the LORD is perfect,
    refreshing the soul;
The decree of the LORD is trustworthy,
    giving wisdom to the simple.

The precepts of the LORD are right,
    rejoicing the heart;
The command of the LORD is clear,
    enlightening the eye.

The fear of the LORD is pure,
    enduring forever;
The ordinances of the LORD are true,
    all of them just.

Let the words of my mouth and the thought of my heart
    find favor before you,
O LORD, my rock and my redeemer.

From Psalm 19

Living the Word This Week

How can I make my life a gift for others in charity?

Spend time each day this week reading Sacred Scripture and meditating on its meaning.

January 30, 2022

Lectio Divina for the Fourth Week in Ordinary Time

We begin our prayer:

In the name of the Father, and of the Son, and of the Holy Spirit. Amen.

Grant us, Lord our God,
that we may honor you with all our mind,
and love everyone in truth of heart.
Through our Lord Jesus Christ, your Son,
who lives and reigns with you in the unity of the Holy Spirit,
God, for ever and ever.

Collect, Fourth Sunday in Ordinary Time

Reading (*Lectio*)

Read the following Scripture two or three times.

Luke 4:21-30

Jesus began speaking in the synagogue, saying: "Today this Scripture passage is fulfilled in your hearing." And all spoke highly of him and were amazed at the gracious words that came from his mouth. They also asked, "Isn't this the son of Joseph?" He said to them, "Surely you will quote me this proverb, 'Physician, cure yourself,' and say, 'Do here in your native place the things that we heard were done in Capernaum.'" And he said, "Amen, I say to you, no prophet is accepted in his own native place. Indeed, I tell you, there were many widows in Israel in the days of Elijah when the sky was closed for three and a half years and a severe famine spread over the entire land. It was to none of these that Elijah was sent, but only to a widow in Zarephath in the land of Sidon. Again, there were many lepers in Israel during the time of Elisha the prophet; yet not one of them was cleansed, but only Naaman the Syrian." When the people in the synagogue heard this, they were all filled with fury. They rose up, drove him out of the town, and led him to the brow of the hill on which their town had been built, to hurl him down headlong. But Jesus passed through the midst of them and went away.

Meditation (*Meditatio*)

After the reading, take some time to reflect in silence on one or more of the following questions:

- What word or words in this passage caught your attention?
- What in this passage comforted you?
- What in this passage challenged you?

If practicing lectio divina as a family or in a group, after the reflection time, invite the participants to share their responses.

Prayer (*Oratio*)

Read the scripture passage one more time. Bring to the Lord the praise, petition, or thanksgiving that the Word inspires in you.

Contemplation (*Contemplatio*)

Read the Scripture again, followed by this reflection:

≈ What conversion of mind, heart, and life is the Lord asking of me?

_____

_____

_____

_____

≈ *Physician, cure yourself.* When have I depended too much on my own strength and abilities? How can I rely more fully on Jesus' healing presence?

_____

_____

_____

_____

≈ *No prophet is accepted in his own native place.* When have I felt rejected because of my faith? When have I shut out others who speak the truth to me?

_____

_____

_____

_____

≈ *Jesus passed through the midst of them and went away.* When have I needed to walk away from things that would upset my spirit? How can I avoid people and places that are near occasions of sin?

_____

_____

_____

_____

≈ *After a period of silent reflection and/or discussion, all recite the Lord's Prayer and the following:*

Closing Prayer

In you, O LORD, I take refuge;
    let me never be put to shame.
In your justice rescue me, and deliver me;
    incline your ear to me, and save me.

Be my rock of refuge,
    a stronghold to give me safety,
    for you are my rock and my fortress.
O my God, rescue me from the hand of the wicked.

For you are my hope, O Lord;
    my trust, O God, from my youth.
On you I depend from birth;
    from my mother's womb you are my strength.

My mouth shall declare your justice,
    day by day your salvation.
O God, you have taught me from my youth,
    and till the present I proclaim your wondrous deeds.

From Psalm 71

Living the Word This Week

How can I make my life a gift for others in charity?

Research parish and diocesan efforts to reach out to the poor, to refugees, and to the incarcerated. Prayerfully discern how you might contribute to these efforts.

February 6, 2022

Lectio Divina for the Fifth Week in Ordinary Time

We begin our prayer:

In the name of the Father, and of the Son, and of the Holy Spirit. Amen.

Keep your family safe, O Lord, with unfailing care,
that, relying solely on the hope of heavenly grace,
they may be defended always by your protection.
Through our Lord Jesus Christ, your Son,
who lives and reigns with you in the unity of the Holy Spirit,
God, for ever and ever.

Collect, Fifth Sunday in Ordinary Time

Reading (*Lectio*)

Read the following Scripture two or three times.

Luke 5:1-11

> While the crowd was pressing in on Jesus and listening to the word
> of God, he was standing by the Lake of Gennesaret. He saw two
> boats there alongside the lake; the fishermen had disembarked
> and were washing their nets. Getting into one of the boats, the
> one belonging to Simon, he asked him to put out a short distance
> from the shore. Then he sat down and taught the crowds from
> the boat. After he had finished speaking, he said to Simon, "Put
> out into deep water and lower your nets for a catch." Simon said
> in reply, "Master, we have worked hard all night and have caught
> nothing, but at your command I will lower the nets." When they
> had done this, they caught a great number of fish and their nets
> were tearing. They signaled to their partners in the other boat to
> come to help them. They came and filled both boats so that the
> boats were in danger of sinking. When Simon Peter saw this, he
> fell at the knees of Jesus and said, "Depart from me, Lord, for I am
> a sinful man." For astonishment at the catch of fish they had made
> seized him and all those with him, and likewise James and John,
> the sons of Zebedee, who were partners of Simon. Jesus said to
> Simon, "Do not be afraid; from now on you will be catching men."
> When they brought their boats to the shore, they left everything
> and followed him.

Meditation (*Meditatio*)

After the reading, take some time to reflect in silence on one or more of the following questions:

- What word or words in this passage caught your attention?
- What in this passage comforted you?
- What in this passage challenged you?

If practicing lectio divina as a family or in a group, after the reflection time, invite the participants to share their responses.

Prayer (*Oratio*)

Read the scripture passage one more time. Bring to the Lord the praise, petition, or thanksgiving that the Word inspires in you.

Contemplation (*Contemplatio*)

Read the Scripture again, followed by this reflection:

∾ What conversion of mind, heart, and life is the Lord asking of me?

_____

_____

_____

_____

~ *The crowd was pressing in on Jesus and listening to the word of God.*
When have I been eager to hear the word of God? How can I be more
enthusiastic about learning and sharing my faith?

_____

_____

_____

_____

~ *Master, we have worked hard all night and have caught nothing, but at
your command I will lower the nets.* When have I felt that my efforts are
in vain? When have I felt that Jesus is supporting me in those efforts?

_____

_____

_____

_____

~ *They left everything and followed him.* What prevents me from following
Jesus more closely? What sinful behaviors do I need to abandon?

_____

_____

_____

_____

Closing Prayer

I will give thanks to you, O Lord, with all my heart,
    for you have heard the words of my mouth;
      in the presence of the angels I will sing your praise;
I will worship at your holy temple
    and give thanks to your name.

Because of your kindness and your truth;
    for you have made great above all things
    your name and your promise.
When I called, you answered me;
    you built up strength within me.

All the kings of the earth shall give thanks to you, O Lord,
    when they hear the words of your mouth;
and they shall sing of the ways of the Lord:
    "Great is the glory of the Lord."

Your right hand saves me.
    The Lord will complete what he has done for me;
your kindness, O Lord endures forever;
    forsake not the work of your hands.

From Psalm 138

Living the Word This Week

How can I make my life a gift for others in charity?

Pray for those who are discerning a vocation to the priesthood, diaconate, or consecrated life.

February 13, 2022

Lectio Divina for the Sixth Week in Ordinary Time

We begin our prayer:

In the name of the Father, and of the Son, and of the Holy Spirit. Amen.

O God, who teach us that you abide
in hearts that are just and true,
grant that we may be so fashioned by your grace
as to become a dwelling pleasing to you.
Through our Lord Jesus Christ, your Son,
who lives and reigns with you in the unity of the Holy Spirit,
God, for ever and ever.

Collect, Sixth Sunday in Ordinary Time

Reading (*Lectio*)

Read the following Scripture two or three times.

Luke 6:17, 20-26

Jesus came down with the twelve and stood on a stretch of level ground with a great crowd of his disciples and a large number of the people from all Judea and Jerusalem and the coastal region of Tyre and Sidon. And raising his eyes toward his disciples he said:

"Blessed are you who are poor,
for the kingdom of God is yours.
Blessed are you who are now hungry,
for you will be satisfied.
Blessed are you who are now weeping,
for you will laugh.
Blessed are you when people hate you,
and when they exclude and insult you,
and denounce your name as evil
on account of the Son of Man.

Rejoice and leap for joy on that day! Behold, your reward will be great in heaven. For their ancestors treated the prophets in the same way.
But woe to you who are rich,
for you have received your consolation.
Woe to you who are filled now,
for you will be hungry.
Woe to you who laugh now,
for you will grieve and weep.
Woe to you when all speak well of you,
for their ancestors treated the false prophets in this way."

Meditation (*Meditatio*)

After the reading, take some time to reflect in silence on one or more of the following questions:

- What word or words in this passage caught your attention?
- What in this passage comforted you?
- What in this passage challenged you?

If practicing lectio divina as a family or in a group, after the reflection time, invite the participants to share their responses.

Prayer (*Oratio*)

Read the scripture passage one more time. Bring to the Lord the praise, petition, or thanksgiving that the Word inspires in you.

Contemplation (*Contemplatio*)

Read the Scripture again, followed by this reflection:

～ What conversion of mind, heart, and life is the Lord asking of me?

_____

_____

_____

_____

~ *Blessed are you who are now weeping, / for you will laugh.* What burdens or circumstances in life grieve me? What things in life bring me joy?

_____

_____

_____

_____

~ *Behold, your reward will be great in heaven.* What reward do I seek from God? What do I imagine that heaven will be like?

_____

_____

_____

_____

~ *Woe to you when all speak well of you, / for their ancestors treated the false prophets in this way.* When have I pursued others' good opinion of me rather than what was right? How do I treat those who speak uncomfortable truths?

_____

_____

_____

_____

~ After a period of silent reflection and/or discussion, all recite the Lord's Prayer and the following:

Closing Prayer

Blessed the man who follows not
    the counsel of the wicked,
nor walks in the way of sinners,
    nor sits in the company of the insolent,
but delights in the law of the LORD
    and meditates on his law day and night.

He is like a tree
    planted near running water,
that yields its fruit in due season,
    and whose leaves never fade.
Whatever he does, prospers.

Not so the wicked, not so;
    they are like chaff which the wind drives away.
For the LORD watches over the way of the just,
    but the way of the wicked vanishes.

From Psalm 1

Living the Word This Week

How can I make my life a gift for others in charity?

Pray for those who have died, especially those who have no one to pray for them.

February 20, 2022

Lectio Divina for the Seventh Week in Ordinary Time

We begin our prayer:

In the name of the Father, and of the Son, and of the Holy Spirit. Amen.

Grant, we pray, almighty God,
that, always pondering spiritual things,
we may carry out in both word and deed
that which is pleasing to you.
Through our Lord Jesus Christ, your Son,
who lives and reigns with you in the unity of the Holy Spirit,
God, for ever and ever.

Collect, Seventh Sunday in Ordinary Time

Reading (*Lectio*)

Read the following Scripture two or three times.

Luke 6:27-38

Jesus said to his disciples: "To you who hear I say, love your enemies, do good to those who hate you, bless those who curse you, pray for those who mistreat you. To the person who strikes you on one cheek, offer the other one as well, and from the person who takes your cloak, do not withhold even your tunic. Give to everyone who asks of you, and from the one who takes what is yours do not demand it back. Do to others as you would have them do to you. For if you love those who love you, what credit is that to you? Even sinners love those who love them. And if you do good to those who do good to you, what credit is that to you? Even sinners do the same. If you lend money to those from whom you expect repayment, what credit is that to you? Even sinners lend to sinners, and get back the same amount. But rather, love your enemies and do good to them, and lend expecting nothing back; then your reward will be great and you will be children of the Most High, for he himself is kind to the ungrateful and the wicked. Be merciful, just as your Father is merciful.

"Stop judging and you will not be judged. Stop condemning and you will not be condemned. Forgive and you will be forgiven. Give, and gifts will be given to you; a good measure, packed together, shaken down, and overflowing, will be poured into your lap. For the measure with which you measure will in return be measured out to you."

Meditation (*Meditatio*)

After the reading, take some time to reflect in silence on one or more of the following questions:

- What word or words in this passage caught your attention?
- What in this passage comforted you?
- What in this passage challenged you?

If practicing lectio divina as a family or in a group, after the reflection time, invite the participants to share their responses.

Prayer (*Oratio*)

Read the scripture passage one more time. Bring to the Lord the praise, petition, or thanksgiving that the Word inspires in you.

Contemplation (*Contemplatio*)

Read the Scripture again, followed by this reflection:

≈ What conversion of mind, heart, and life is the Lord asking of me?

_____

_____

_____

_____

~ *Bless those who curse you, pray for those who mistreat you.* Who has hurt me or mistreated me in some way? How can I pray for this person?

_____

_____

_____

_____

~ *Forgive and you will be forgiven.* Whom do I need to forgive? From whom do I need to seek forgiveness?

_____

_____

_____

_____

~ *For the measure with which you measure will in return be measured out to you.* How often do I hold myself and others to unrealistic standards? How can I be more generous with others and with myself?

_____

_____

_____

_____

~ *After a period of silent reflection and/or discussion, all recite the Lord's Prayer and the following:*

Closing Prayer

Bless the LORD, O my soul;
    and all my being, bless his holy name.
Bless the LORD, O my soul,
    and forget not all his benefits.

He pardons all your iniquities,
    heals all your ills.
He redeems your life from destruction,
    crowns you with kindness and compassion.

Merciful and gracious is the LORD,
    slow to anger and abounding in kindness.
Not according to our sins does he deal with us,
    nor does he requite us according to our crimes.

As far as the east is from the west,
    so far has he put our transgressions from us.
As a father has compassion on his children,
    so the LORD has compassion on those who fear him.

From Psalm 103

Living the Word This Week

How can I make my life a gift for others in charity?

Prayerfully consider how you can share your gifts of time, talent, and treasure with those in need.

February 27, 2022

Lectio Divina for the Eighth Week in Ordinary Time

We begin our prayer:

In the name of the Father, and of the Son, and of the Holy Spirit. Amen.

Grant us, O Lord, we pray,
that the course of our world
may be directed by your peaceful rule
and that your Church may rejoice,
untroubled in her devotion.
Through our Lord Jesus Christ, your Son,
who lives and reigns with you in the unity of the Holy Spirit,
God, for ever and ever.

Collect, Eighth Sunday in Ordinary Time

Reading (*Lectio*)

Read the following Scripture two or three times.

Luke 6:39-45

> Jesus told his disciples a parable, "Can a blind person guide a blind person? Will not both fall into a pit? No disciple is superior to the teacher; but when fully trained, every disciple will be like his teacher. Why do you notice the splinter in your brother's eye, but do not perceive the wooden beam in your own? How can you say to your brother, 'Brother, let me remove that splinter in your eye,' when you do not even notice the wooden beam in your own eye? You hypocrite! Remove the wooden beam from your eye first; then you will see clearly to remove the splinter in your brother's eye.

> "A good tree does not bear rotten fruit, nor does a rotten tree bear good fruit. For every tree is known by its own fruit. For people do not pick figs from thornbushes, nor do they gather grapes from brambles. A good person out of the store of goodness in his heart produces good, but an evil person out of a store of evil produces evil; for from the fullness of the heart the mouth speaks."

Meditation (*Meditatio*)

After the reading, take some time to reflect in silence on one or more of the following questions:

- What word or words in this passage caught your attention?
- What in this passage comforted you?
- What in this passage challenged you?

If practicing lectio divina as a family or in a group, after the reflection time, invite the participants to share their responses.

Prayer (*Oratio*)

Read the scripture passage one more time. Bring to the Lord the praise, petition, or thanksgiving that the Word inspires in you.

Contemplation (*Contemplatio*)

Read the Scripture again, followed by this reflection:

≈ What conversion of mind, heart, and life is the Lord asking of me?

_____

_____

_____

_____

≈ *When fully trained, every disciple will be like his teacher.* What teachers have helped to shape my faith? How can I become more like Jesus?

_____

_____

_____

_____

∼ *Remove the wooden beam from your eye first; then you will see clearly to remove the splinter in your brother's eye.* What beam do I need to remove from my eye? How can I learn to see my brothers and sisters with the eyes of faith?

_____

_____

_____

_____

∼ *For every tree is known by its own fruit.* By what fruit am I known? What spiritual fruits do I wish to cultivate in my life?

_____

_____

_____

_____

∼ *After a period of silent reflection and/or discussion, all recite the Lord's Prayer and the following:*

Closing Prayer

It is good to give thanks to the LORD,
    to sing praise to your name, Most High,
To proclaim your kindness at dawn
    and your faithfulness throughout the night.

The just one shall flourish like the palm tree,
    like a cedar of Lebanon shall he grow.
They that are planted in the house of the LORD
    shall flourish in the courts of our God.

They shall bear fruit even in old age;
    vigorous and sturdy shall they be,
Declaring how just is the LORD,
    my rock, in whom there is no wrong.

From Psalm 92

Living the Word This Week

How can I make my life a gift for others in charity?

Commit to some time for spiritual reading (the Bible, the lives of the saints, the *Catechism*, papal documents, etc.) each day during Lent.

March 2, 2022

Lectio Divina for Ash Wednesday

We begin our prayer:

In the name of the Father, and of the Son, and of the Holy Spirit. Amen.

Prompt our actions with your inspiration, we pray, O Lord,
and further them with your constant help,
that all we do may always begin from you
and by you be brought to completion.
Through our Lord Jesus Christ, your Son,
who lives and reigns with you in the unity of the Holy Spirit,
God, for ever and ever.

Collect, Thursday after Ash Wednesday

Reading (*Lectio*)

Read the following Scripture two or three times.

Matthew 6:1-6, 16-18

> Jesus said to his disciples: "Take care not to perform righteous
> deeds in order that people may see them; otherwise, you will have

no recompense from your heavenly Father. When you give alms, do not blow a trumpet before you, as the hypocrites do in the synagogues and in the streets to win the praise of others. Amen, I say to you, they have received their reward. But when you give alms, do not let your left hand know what your right is doing, so that your almsgiving may be secret. And your Father who sees in secret will repay you.

"When you pray, do not be like the hypocrites, who love to stand and pray in the synagogues and on street corners so that others may see them. Amen, I say to you, they have received their reward. But when you pray, go to your inner room, close the door, and pray to your Father in secret. And your Father who sees in secret will repay you.

"When you fast, do not look gloomy like the hypocrites. They neglect their appearance, so that they may appear to others to be fasting. Amen, I say to you, they have received their reward. But when you fast, anoint your head and wash your face, so that you may not appear to be fasting, except to your Father who is hidden. And your Father who sees what is hidden will repay you."

Meditation (*Meditatio*)

After the reading, take some time to reflect in silence on one or more of the following questions:

- What word or words in this passage caught your attention?
- What in this passage comforted you?
- What in this passage challenged you?

If practicing lectio divina as a family or in a group, after the reflection time, invite the participants to share their responses.

Prayer (*Oratio*)

Read the scripture passage one more time. Bring to the Lord the praise, petition, or thanksgiving that the Word inspires in you.

Contemplation (*Contemplatio*)

Read the Scripture again, followed by this reflection:

∾ What conversion of mind, heart, and life is the Lord asking of me?

_____

_____

_____

_____

∾ *When you give alms, do not blow a trumpet before you, as the hypocrites do in the synagogues and in the streets to win the praise of others.* When have I sought attention for doing good? How often does the good opinion of others motivate my actions?

_____

_____

_____

_____

∾ *Amen, I say to you, they have received their reward.* What reward do I hope to receive from living my faith? What rewards have I already received from living my faith?

_____

_____

_____

_____

∾ *But when you fast, anoint your head and wash your face, so that you may not appear to be fasting, except to your Father who is hidden.* How do I communicate to others the joy that faith in Christ and his Church bring me? How can I share that joy with others?

_____

_____

_____

_____

∾ *After a period of silent reflection and/or discussion, all recite the Lord's Prayer and the following:*

Closing Prayer

Have mercy on me, O God, in your goodness;
 in the greatness of your compassion wipe out my offense.
Thoroughly wash me from my guilt
 and of my sin cleanse me.

For I acknowledge my offense,
 and my sin is before me always:
"Against you only have I sinned,
 and done what is evil in your sight."

A clean heart create for me, O God,
 and a steadfast spirit renew within me.
Cast me not out from your presence,
 and your Holy Spirit take not from me.

Give me back the joy of your salvation,
 and a willing spirit sustain in me.
O Lord, open my lips,
 and my mouth shall proclaim your praise.

From Psalm 51

Living the Word This Week

How can I make my life a gift for others in charity?

Decide how you will observe Lent with practices of prayer, fasting, and almsgiving.

March 6, 2022

Lectio Divina for the First Week of Lent

We begin our prayer:

In the name of the Father, and of the Son, and of the Holy Spirit. Amen.

Turn our hearts to you, eternal Father,
and grant that, seeking always the one thing necessary
and carrying out works of charity,
we may be dedicated to your worship.
Through our Lord Jesus Christ, your Son,
who lives and reigns with you in the unity of the Holy Spirit,
God, for ever and ever.

Collect, Saturday of the First Week of Lent

Reading (*Lectio*)

Read the following Scripture two or three times.

Luke 4:1-13

Filled with the Holy Spirit, Jesus returned from the Jordan and
was led by the Spirit into the desert for forty days, to be tempted

by the devil. He ate nothing during those days, and when they were over he was hungry. The devil said to him, "If you are the Son of God, command this stone to become bread." Jesus answered him, "It is written, *One does not live on bread alone.*" Then he took him up and showed him all the kingdoms of the world in a single instant. The devil said to him, "I shall give to you all this power and glory; for it has been handed over to me, and I may give it to whomever I wish. All this will be yours, if you worship me." Jesus said to him in reply, "It is written:

You shall worship the Lord, your God,
*   and him alone shall you serve."*

Then he led him to Jerusalem, made him stand on the parapet of the temple, and said to him, "If you are the Son of God, throw yourself down from here, for it is written:

He will command his angels concerning you, to guard you,

   and:

With their hands they will support you,
lest you dash your foot against a stone."

Jesus said to him in reply,

   "It also says,

You shall not put the Lord, your God, to the test."

When the devil had finished every temptation, he departed from him for a time.

Meditation (*Meditatio*)

After the reading, take some time to reflect in silence on one or more of the following questions:

- What word or words in this passage caught your attention?
- What in this passage comforted you?
- What in this passage challenged you?

If practicing lectio divina as a family or in a group, after the reflection time, invite the participants to share their responses.

Prayer (*Oratio*)

Read the scripture passage one more time. Bring to the Lord the praise, petition, or thanksgiving that the Word inspires in you.

Contemplation (*Contemplatio*)

Read the Scripture again, followed by this reflection:

≈ What conversion of mind, heart, and life is the Lord asking of me?

_____

_____

_____

_____

~ *He ate nothing during those days, and when they were over he was hungry.* For what do I hunger? How can I better nourish my soul?

_____

_____

_____

_____

~ *You shall worship the Lord, your God, | and him alone shall you serve.* What distracts me from worshiping the Lord? How can I serve the Lord more faithfully and wholeheartedly?

_____

_____

_____

_____

~ *With their hands they will support you, | lest you dash your foot against a stone.* What stones or stumbling blocks endanger me? How do I experience God's loving support?

_____

_____

_____

_____

∼ After a period of silent reflection and/or discussion, all recite the Lord's Prayer and the following:

Closing Prayer

You who dwell in the shelter of the Most High,
who abide in the shadow of the Almighty,
say to the LORD, "My refuge and fortress,
my God in whom I trust."

No evil shall befall you,
nor shall affliction come near your tent,
For to his angels he has given command about you,
that they guard you in all your ways.

Upon their hands they shall bear you up,
lest you dash your foot against a stone.
You shall tread upon the asp and the viper;
you shall trample down the lion and the dragon.

Because he clings to me, I will deliver him;
I will set him on high because he acknowledges my name.
He shall call upon me, and I will answer him;
I will be with him in distress;
I will deliver him and glorify him.

From Psalm 91

Living the Word This Week

How can I make my life a gift for others in charity?

Make a special effort to be fully present and attentive in prayer and at the liturgy this week.

March 13, 2022

Lectio Divina for the Second Week of Lent

We begin our prayer:

In the name of the Father, and of the Son, and of the Holy Spirit. Amen.

Keep your family, O Lord,
schooled always in good works,
and so comfort them with your protection here
as to lead them graciously to gifts on high.
Through our Lord Jesus Christ, your Son,
who lives and reigns with you in the unity of the Holy Spirit,
God, for ever and ever.

Collect, Wednesday of the Second Week of Lent

Reading (*Lectio*)

Read the following Scripture two or three times.

Luke 9:28b-36

> Jesus took Peter, John, and James and went up the mountain to
> pray. While he was praying his face changed in appearance and

his clothing became dazzling white. And behold, two men were conversing with him, Moses and Elijah, who appeared in glory and spoke of his exodus that he was going to accomplish in Jerusalem. Peter and his companions had been overcome by sleep, but becoming fully awake, they saw his glory and the two men standing with him. As they were about to part from him, Peter said to Jesus, "Master, it is good that we are here; let us make three tents, one for you, one for Moses, and one for Elijah." But he did not know what he was saying. While he was still speaking, a cloud came and cast a shadow over them, and they became frightened when they entered the cloud. Then from the cloud came a voice that said, "This is my chosen Son; listen to him." After the voice had spoken, Jesus was found alone. They fell silent and did not at that time tell anyone what they had seen.

Meditation (*Meditatio*)

After the reading, take some time to reflect in silence on one or more of the following questions:

- What word or words in this passage caught your attention?
- What in this passage comforted you?
- What in this passage challenged you?

If practicing lectio divina as a family or in a group, after the reflection time, invite the participants to share their responses.

Prayer (*Oratio*)

Read the scripture passage one more time. Bring to the Lord the praise, petition, or thanksgiving that the Word inspires in you.

Contemplation (*Contemplatio*)

Read the Scripture again, followed by this reflection:

∾ What conversion of mind, heart, and life is the Lord asking of me?

_____

_____

_____

_____

∾ *While he was praying his face changed in appearance.* For what do I need to pray? How has prayer changed me?

_____

_____

_____

_____

∾ *Peter and his companions had been overcome by sleep.* What overcomes my desire to follow Jesus? How can I wake up to what God wants from me?

_____

_____

_____

_____

≈ *Master, it is good that we are here.* Where is God calling me to be? Whom has God placed in my life to help me?

_____

_____

_____

_____

≈ *After a period of silent reflection and/or discussion, all recite the Lord's Prayer and the following:*

Closing Prayer

The LORD is my light and my salvation;
    whom should I fear?
The LORD is my life's refuge;
    of whom should I be afraid?

Hear, O LORD, the sound of my call;
    have pity on me, and answer me.
Of you my heart speaks; you my glance seeks.

Your presence, O LORD, I seek.
    Hide not your face from me;
do not in anger repel your servant.
    You are my helper: cast me not off.

I believe that I shall see the bounty of the Lord
    in the land of the living.
Wait for the Lord with courage;
    be stouthearted, and wait for the Lord.

From Psalm 27

Living the Word This Week

How can I make my life a gift for others in charity?

Make a good examination of conscience and plan to receive the Sacrament of Penance this Lent.

March 19, 2022

Lectio Divina for the Solemnity of Saint Joseph

We begin our prayer:

In the name of the Father, and of the Son, and of the Holy Spirit. Amen.

Grant, we pray, almighty God,
that by Saint Joseph's intercession
your Church may constantly watch over
the unfolding of the mysteries of human salvation,
whose beginnings you entrusted to his faithful care.
Through our Lord Jesus Christ, your Son,
who lives and reigns with you in the unity of the Holy Spirit,
God, for ever and ever.

Collect, Solemnity of Saint Joseph

Reading (*Lectio*)

Read the following Scripture two or three times.

Matthew 1:16, 18-21, 24a

Jacob was the father of Joseph, the husband of Mary. Of her was born Jesus who is called the Christ.

Now this is how the birth of Jesus Christ came about. When his mother Mary was betrothed to Joseph, but before they lived together, she was found with child through the Holy Spirit. Joseph her husband, since he was a righteous man, yet unwilling to expose her to shame, decided to divorce her quietly. Such was his intention when, behold, the angel of the Lord appeared to him in a dream and said, "Joseph, son of David, do not be afraid to take Mary your wife into your home. For it is through the Holy Spirit that this child has been conceived in her. She will bear a son and you are to name him Jesus, because he will save his people from their sins." When Joseph awoke, he did as the angel of the Lord had commanded him and took his wife into his home.

Meditation (*Meditatio*)

After the reading, take some time to reflect in silence on one or more of the following questions:

- What word or words in this passage caught your attention?
- What in this passage comforted you?
- What in this passage challenged you?

If practicing lectio divina as a family or in a group, after the reflection time, invite the participants to share their responses.

Prayer (*Oratio*)

Read the scripture passage one more time. Bring to the Lord the praise, petition, or thanksgiving that the Word inspires in you.

Contemplation (*Contemplatio*)

Read the Scripture again, followed by this reflection:

~ What conversion of mind, heart, and life is the Lord asking of me?

_____

_____

_____

_____

~ *Behold, the angel of the Lord appeared to him in a dream.* When have I felt the presence of the Lord? When have I heard God calling me?

_____

_____

_____

_____

∼ *Do not be afraid.* Of what am I afraid? How do my fears keep me from living as a disciple?

_____

_____

_____

_____

∼ *He did as the angel of the Lord had commanded him.* When have I followed the Lord's command? When have I failed to follow his command?

_____

_____

_____

_____

∼ *After a period of silent reflection and/or discussion, all recite the Lord's Prayer and the following:*

Closing Prayer

The promises of the LORD I will sing forever;
>through all generations my mouth shall proclaim your faithfulness,
For you have said, "My kindness is established forever";
>in heaven you have confirmed your faithfulness.

"I have made a covenant with my chosen one,
    I have sworn to David my servant:
Forever will I confirm your posterity
    and establish your throne for all generations."

"He shall say of me, 'You are my father,
    my God, the Rock, my savior.'
Forever I will maintain my kindness toward him,
    and my covenant with him stands firm."

From Psalm 89

Living the Word This Week

How can I make my life a gift for others in charity?

Read chapter 5 of Pope Francis's Apostolic Exhortation *Amoris Laetitia*: *www.vatican.va/content/dam/francesco/pdf/apost_exhortations/documents/ papa-francesco_esortazione-ap_20160319_amoris-laetitia_en.pdf.*

March 20, 2022

Lectio Divina for the Third Week of Lent

We begin our prayer:

In the name of the Father, and of the Son, and of the Holy Spirit. Amen.

May your unfailing compassion, O Lord,
cleanse and protect your Church,
and, since without you she cannot stand secure,
may she be always governed by your grace.
Through our Lord Jesus Christ, your Son,
who lives and reigns with you in the unity of the Holy Spirit,
God, for ever and ever.

Collect, Monday of the Third Week of Lent

Reading (*Lectio*)

Read the following Scripture two or three times.

Luke 13:1-9

> Some people told Jesus about the Galileans whose blood Pilate
> had mingled with the blood of their sacrifices. Jesus said to them

in reply, "Do you think that because these Galileans suffered in this way they were greater sinners than all other Galileans? By no means! But I tell you, if you do not repent, you will all perish as they did! Or those eighteen people who were killed when the tower at Siloam fell on them—do you think they were more guilty than everyone else who lived in Jerusalem? By no means! But I tell you, if you do not repent, you will all perish as they did!"

And he told them this parable: "There once was a person who had a fig tree planted in his orchard, and when he came in search of fruit on it but found none, he said to the gardener, 'For three years now I have come in search of fruit on this fig tree but have found none. So cut it down. Why should it exhaust the soil?' He said to him in reply, 'Sir, leave it for this year also, and I shall cultivate the ground around it and fertilize it; it may bear fruit in the future. If not you can cut it down.'"

Meditation (*Meditatio*)

After the reading, take some time to reflect in silence on one or more of the following questions:

- What word or words in this passage caught your attention?
- What in this passage comforted you?
- What in this passage challenged you?

If practicing lectio divina as a family or in a group, after the reflection time, invite the participants to share their responses.

Prayer (*Oratio*)

Read the scripture passage one more time. Bring to the Lord the praise, petition, or thanksgiving that the Word inspires in you.

Contemplation (*Contemplatio*)

Read the Scripture again, followed by this reflection:

∾ What conversion of mind, heart, and life is the Lord asking of me?

_____

_____

_____

_____

∾ *Do you think that because these Galileans suffered in this way they were greater sinners than all other Galileans?* How do I show compassion to those who are suffering? How often do I focus on the sins of others rather than on my own need for repentance?

_____

_____

_____

_____

~ *Why should it exhaust the soil?* What things deplete my commitment to my faith? How can I better nourish the soil of my faith?

_____

_____

_____

_____

~ *Sir, leave it for this year also, and I shall cultivate the ground around it.* What changes in my faith practice have I been procrastinating about (e.g., returning to the Sacrament of Penance, attending daily Mass, more regular prayer, more works of mercy)? How can I cultivate these practices with greater commitment?

_____

_____

_____

_____

~ *After a period of silent reflection and/or discussion, all recite the Lord's Prayer and the following:*

Closing Prayer

Bless the LORD, O my soul;
    and all my being, bless his holy name.
Bless the LORD, O my soul,
    and forget not all his benefits.

He pardons all your iniquities,
    heals all your ills,
He redeems your life from destruction,
    crowns you with kindness and compassion.

The LORD secures justice
    and the rights of all the oppressed.
He has made known his ways to Moses,
    and his deeds to the children of Israel.

Merciful and gracious is the LORD,
    slow to anger and abounding in kindness.
For as the heavens are high above the earth,
    so surpassing is his kindness toward those who fear him.

From Psalm 103

Living the Word This Week

How can I make my life a gift for others in charity?

Commit to one new spiritual practice for the rest of Lent.

March 27, 2022

Lectio Divina for the Fourth Week of Lent

We begin our prayer:

In the name of the Father, and of the Son, and of the Holy Spirit. Amen.

O God, who have prepared
fitting helps for us in our weakness,
grant, we pray, that we may receive
their healing effects with joy
and reflect them in a holy way of life.
Through our Lord Jesus Christ, your Son,
who lives and reigns with you in the unity of the Holy Spirit,
God, for ever and ever.

Collect, Friday of the Fourth Week of Lent

Reading (*Lectio*)

Read the following Scripture two or three times.

Luke 15:1-3, 11-32

Tax collectors and sinners were all drawing near to listen to Jesus, but the Pharisees and scribes began to complain, saying, "This man welcomes sinners and eats with them." So to them Jesus addressed this parable: "A man had two sons, and the younger son said to his father, 'Father give me the share of your estate that should come to me.' So the father divided the property between them. After a few days, the younger son collected all his belongings and set off to a distant country where he squandered his inheritance on a life of dissipation. When he had freely spent everything, a severe famine struck that country, and he found himself in dire need. So he hired himself out to one of the local citizens who sent him to his farm to tend the swine. And he longed to eat his fill of the pods on which the swine fed, but nobody gave him any. Coming to his senses he thought, 'How many of my father's hired workers have more than enough food to eat, but here am I, dying from hunger. I shall get up and go to my father and I shall say to him, "Father, I have sinned against heaven and against you. I no longer deserve to be called your son; treat me as you would treat one of your hired workers."' So he got up and went back to his father. While he was still a long way off, his father caught sight of him, and was filled with compassion. He ran to his son, embraced him and kissed him. His son said to him, 'Father, I have sinned against heaven and against you; I no longer deserve to be called your son.' But his father ordered his servants, 'Quickly bring the finest robe and put it on him; put a ring on his finger and sandals on his feet. Take the fattened calf and slaughter it. Then let us celebrate with a feast, because this son of mine was dead, and has come to life again; he was lost, and has been found.' Then the celebration began. Now the older son had been out in the field and, on his way back, as he neared the house, he heard the sound of music and dancing. He called one of the servants and asked what this might mean. The servant said to him, 'Your brother has returned and your father has slaughtered the fattened calf because he has him back safe and sound.' He became angry, and when he refused to enter the house, his father came out and pleaded with him. He said to his father in reply, 'Look, all these years I served you and not once did I disobey your orders; yet you never gave me even a young goat to feast on with my friends. But when your son returns who swallowed up your property with prostitutes, for him you slaughter the fattened calf.' He said to him, 'My son, you are here with me always; everything I have is yours. But now we must celebrate and rejoice, because your brother was dead and has come to life again; he was lost and has been found.'"

Meditation (*Meditatio*)

After the reading, take some time to reflect in silence on one or more of the following questions:

- What word or words in this passage caught your attention?
- What in this passage comforted you?
- What in this passage challenged you?

If practicing lectio divina as a family or in a group, after the reflection time, invite the participants to share their responses.

Prayer (*Oratio*)

Read the scripture passage one more time. Bring to the Lord the praise, petition, or thanksgiving that the Word inspires in you.

Contemplation (*Contemplatio*)

Read the Scripture again, followed by this reflection:

≈ What conversion of mind, heart, and life is the Lord asking of me?

\
\
\
\

≈ *Tax collectors and sinners were all drawing near to listen to Jesus.* When have I helped others draw near to listen to Jesus? When have I been an obstacle to their drawing near?

\
\
\
\

≈ *He squandered his inheritance on a life of dissipation. . . . and he found himself in dire need.* When have I squandered the gift of my faith? What do I need to grow in faith?

_____

_____

_____

_____

≈ *This son of mine was dead, and has come to life again; he was lost, and has been found.* When have I felt lost or dead in my spiritual life? What has been life-giving for me?

_____

_____

_____

_____

≈ *After a period of silent reflection and/or discussion, all recite the Lord's Prayer and the following:*

Closing Prayer

I will bless the LORD at all times;
    his praise shall be ever in my mouth.
Let my soul glory in the LORD;
    the lowly will hear me and be glad.

Glorify the LORD with me,
let us together extol his name.
I sought the LORD, and he answered me
and delivered me from all my fears.

Look to him that you may be radiant with joy,
and your faces may not blush with shame.
When the poor one called out, the LORD heard,
and from all his distress he saved him.

From Psalm 34

Living the Word This Week

How can I make my life a gift for others in charity?

Invite someone to come to church with you for a liturgy, a devotion, a faith formation class, or a service project.

April 3, 2022

Lectio Divina for the Fifth Week of Lent

We begin our prayer:

In the name of the Father, and of the Son, and of the Holy Spirit. Amen.

Enlighten, O God of compassion,
the hearts of your children, sanctified by penance,
and in your kindness
grant those you stir to a sense of devotion
a gracious hearing when they cry out to you.
Through our Lord Jesus Christ, your Son,
who lives and reigns with you in the unity of the Holy Spirit,
God, for ever and ever.

Collect, Wednesday of the Fifth Week of Lent

Reading (*Lectio*)

Read the following Scripture two or three times.

John 8:1-11

Jesus went to the Mount of Olives. But early in the morning he arrived again in the temple area, and all the people started coming to him, and he sat down and taught them. Then the scribes and the Pharisees brought a woman who had been caught in adultery and made her stand in the middle. They said to him, "Teacher, this woman was caught in the very act of committing adultery. Now in the law, Moses commanded us to stone such women. So what do you say?" They said this to test him, so that they could have some charge to bring against him. Jesus bent down and began to write on the ground with his finger. But when they continued asking him, he straightened up and said to them, "Let the one among you who is without sin be the first to throw a stone at her." Again he bent down and wrote on the ground. And in response, they went away one by one, beginning with the elders. So he was left alone with the woman before him. Then Jesus straightened up and said to her, "Woman, where are they? Has no one condemned you?" She replied, "No one, sir." Then Jesus said, "Neither do I condemn you. Go, and from now on do not sin any more."

Meditation (*Meditatio*)

After the reading, take some time to reflect in silence on one or more of the following questions:

- What word or words in this passage caught your attention?
- What in this passage comforted you?
- What in this passage challenged you?

If practicing lectio divina as a family or in a group, after the reflection time, invite the participants to share their responses.

Prayer (*Oratio*)

Read the scripture passage one more time. Bring to the Lord the praise, petition, or thanksgiving that the Word inspires in you.

Contemplation (*Contemplatio*)

Read the Scripture again, followed by this reflection:

≈ What conversion of mind, heart, and life is the Lord asking of me?

_____

_____

_____

_____

≈ *They said this to test him, so that they could have some charge to bring against him.* When have I sought to highlight someone's flaws or errors? How can I meet people with kindness instead of cynicism?

_____

_____

_____

_____

≈ *Beginning with the elders.* How have my elders shared their faith with me? How can I help to pass the faith on to future generations?

_____

_____

_____

_____

≈ *Neither do I condemn you. Go, and from now on do not sin any more.* How have I condemned others? With the help of God's grace, how can I foster repentance and conversion in my life?

_____

_____

_____

_____

≈ *After a period of silent reflection and/or discussion, all recite the Lord's Prayer and the following:*

Closing Prayer

When the LORD brought back the captives of Zion,
    we were like men dreaming.
Then our mouth was filled with laughter,
    and our tongue with rejoicing.

Then they said among the nations,
"The LORD has done great things for them."
The LORD has done great things for us;
we are glad indeed.

Restore our fortunes, O LORD,
like the torrents in the southern desert.
Those that sow in tears
shall reap rejoicing.

Although they go forth weeping,
carrying the seed to be sown,
They shall come back rejoicing,
carrying their sheaves.

From Psalm 126

Living the Word This Week

How can I make my life a gift for others in charity?

In these closing days of Lent, reflect on God's gift of forgiveness: *www.usccb.org/prayer-and-worship/sacraments-and-sacramentals/penance/upload/Penance-Statement-ENG.pdf.*

April 10, 2022

Lectio Divina for Holy Week

We begin our prayer:

In the name of the Father, and of the Son, and of the Holy Spirit. Amen.

Remember your mercies, O Lord,
and with your eternal protection sanctify your servants,
for whom Christ your Son,
by the shedding of his Blood,
established the Paschal Mystery.
Who lives and reigns for ever and ever.

Opening Prayer, Good Friday, first option

Reading (*Lectio*)

Read the following Scripture two or three times.

Luke 23:26-46

> As they led [Jesus] away they took hold of a certain Simon, a Cyrenian, who was coming in from the country; and after laying the cross on him, they made him carry it behind Jesus. A large crowd

of people followed Jesus, including many women who mourned and lamented him. Jesus turned to them and said, "Daughters of Jerusalem, do not weep for me; weep instead for yourselves and for your children for indeed, the days are coming when people will say, 'Blessed are the barren, the wombs that never bore and the breasts that never nursed.' At that time people will say to the mountains, 'Fall upon us!' and to the hills, 'Cover us!' for if these things are done when the wood is green what will happen when it is dry?" Now two others, both criminals, were led away with him to be executed.

When they came to the place called the Skull, they crucified him and the criminals there, one on his right, the other on his left. Then Jesus said, "Father, forgive them, they know not what they do." They divided his garments by casting lots. The people stood by and watched; the rulers, meanwhile, sneered at him and said, "He saved others, let him save himself if he is the chosen one, the Christ of God." Even the soldiers jeered at him. As they approached to offer him wine they called out, "If you are King of the Jews, save yourself." Above him there was an inscription that read, "This is the King of the Jews." Now one of the criminals hanging there reviled Jesus, saying, "Are you not the Christ? Save yourself and us." The other, however, rebuking him, said in reply, "Have you no fear of God, for you are subject to the same condemnation? And indeed, we have been condemned justly, for the sentence we received corresponds to our crimes, but this man has done nothing criminal." Then he said, "Jesus, remember me when you come into your kingdom." He replied to him, "Amen, I say to you, today you will be with me in Paradise."

It was now about noon and darkness came over the whole land until three in the afternoon because of an eclipse of the sun. Then the veil of the temple was torn down the middle. Jesus cried out in a loud voice, "Father, into your hands I commend my spirit"; and when he had said this he breathed his last.

Meditation (*Meditatio*)

After the reading, take some time to reflect in silence on one or more of the following questions:

- What word or words in this passage caught your attention?
- What in this passage comforted you?
- What in this passage challenged you?

If practicing lectio divina as a family or in a group, after the reflection time, invite the participants to share their responses.

Prayer (*Oratio*)

Read the scripture passage one more time. Bring to the Lord the praise, petition, or thanksgiving that the Word inspires in you.

Contemplation (*Contemplatio*)

Read the Scripture again, followed by this reflection:

≈ What conversion of mind, heart, and life is the Lord asking of me?

_____

_____

_____

_____

～ *After laying the cross on him, they made him carry it behind Jesus.* What crosses am I called to bear? How can I help those around me to carry their crosses?

_____

_____

_____

_____

～ *Father, forgive them, they know not what they do.* How have I sinned through ignorance or inattention? How can I foster a spirit of conversion and repentance?

_____

_____

_____

_____

～ *Father, into your hands I commend my spirit.* What cares and concerns do I need to place into the Father's hands? How can I increase in my trust of God's providence?

_____

_____

_____

_____

~ *After a period of silent reflection and/or discussion, all recite the Lord's Prayer and the following:*

Closing Prayer

All who see me scoff at me;
    they mock me with parted lips, they wag their heads:
"He relied on the LORD; let him deliver him,
    let him rescue him, if he loves him."

Indeed, many dogs surround me,
    a pack of evildoers closes in upon me;
They have pierced my hands and my feet;
    I can count all my bones.

They divide my garments among them,
    and for my vesture they cast lots.
But you, O LORD, be not far from me;
    O my help, hasten to aid me.

I will proclaim your name to my brethren;
    in the midst of the assembly I will praise you:
"You who fear the LORD, praise him;
    all you descendants of Jacob, give glory to him;
    revere him, all you descendants of Israel!"

From Psalm 22

Living the Word This Week

How can I make my life a gift for others in charity?

As much as possible, participate in your parish's celebration of the Paschal Triduum.

April 17, 2022

Lectio Divina for the Octave of Easter

We begin our prayer:

In the name of the Father, and of the Son, and of the Holy Spirit. Amen.

O God, who have united the many nations
in confessing your name,
grant that those reborn in the font of Baptism
may be one in the faith of their hearts
and the homage of their deeds.
Through our Lord Jesus Christ, your Son,
who lives and reigns with you in the unity of the Holy Spirit,
God, for ever and ever.

Collect, Thursday within the Octave of Easter

Reading (*Lectio*)

Read the following Scripture two or three times.

Luke 24:1-12

> At daybreak on the first day of the week the women who had come from Galilee with Jesus took the spices they had prepared and went to the tomb. They found the stone rolled away from the tomb; but when they entered, they did not find the body of the Lord Jesus. While they were puzzling over this, behold, two men in dazzling garments appeared to them. They were terrified and bowed their faces to the ground. They said to them, "Why do you seek the living one among the dead? He is not here, but he has been raised. Remember what he said to you while he was still in Galilee, that the Son of Man must be handed over to sinners and be crucified, and rise on the third day." And they remembered his words. Then they returned from the tomb and announced all these things to the eleven and to all the others. The women were Mary Magdalene, Joanna, and Mary the mother of James; the others who accompanied them also told this to the apostles, but their story seemed like nonsense and they did not believe them. But Peter got up and ran to the tomb, bent down, and saw the burial cloths alone; then he went home amazed at what had happened.

Meditation (*Meditatio*)

After the reading, take some time to reflect in silence on one or more of the following questions:

- What word or words in this passage caught your attention?
- What in this passage comforted you?
- What in this passage challenged you?

If practicing lectio divina as a family or in a group, after the reflection time, invite the participants to share their responses.

Prayer (*Oratio*)

Read the scripture passage one more time. Bring to the Lord the praise, petition, or thanksgiving that the Word inspires in you.

Contemplation (*Contemplatio*)

Read the Scripture again, followed by this reflection:

∾ What conversion of mind, heart, and life is the Lord asking of me?

_____

_____

_____

_____

∾ *They found the stone rolled away from the tomb.* What obstacles keep me from living my faith more fully? How can I begin to remove these obstacles?

_____

_____

_____

_____

∾ *Remember what he said to you.* What prayer or Scripture passage is particularly memorable for me? What people or circumstances help ground me in my faith?

_____

_____

_____

_____

∾ *He went home amazed at what had happened.* When has God's working in my life amazed me? How can I share God's amazing actions with other?

_____

_____

_____

_____

∾ *After a period of silent reflection and/or discussion, all recite the Lord's Prayer and the following:*

Closing Prayer

Give thanks to the LORD, for he is good,
    for his mercy endures forever.
Let the house of Israel say,
    "His mercy endures forever."

"The right hand of the LORD has struck with power;
the right hand of the LORD is exalted.
I shall not die, but live,
and declare the works of the LORD."

The stone which the builders rejected
has become the cornerstone.
By the LORD has this been done;
it is wonderful in our eyes.

From Psalm 118

Living the Word This Week

How can I make my life a gift for others in charity?

Join or start a bible study in your parish.

April 24, 2022

Lectio Divina for the Second Week of Easter

We begin our prayer:

In the name of the Father, and of the Son, and of the Holy Spirit. Amen.

Enable us, we pray, almighty God,
to proclaim the power of the risen Lord,
that we, who have received the pledge of his gift,
may come to possess all he gives
when it is fully revealed.
Through our Lord Jesus Christ, your Son,
who lives and reigns with you in the unity of the Holy Spirit,
God, for ever and ever.

Collect, Tuesday of the Second Week of Easter

Reading (*Lectio*)

Read the following Scripture two or three times.

John 20:19-31

On the evening of that first day of the week, when the doors were locked, where the disciples were, for fear of the Jews, Jesus came and stood in their midst and said to them, "Peace be with you." When he had said this, he showed them his hands and his side. The disciples rejoiced when they saw the Lord. Jesus said to them again, "Peace be with you. As the Father has sent me, so I send you." And when he had said this, he breathed on them and said to them, "Receive the Holy Spirit. Whose sins you forgive are forgiven them, and whose sins you retain are retained."

Thomas, called Didymus, one of the Twelve, was not with them when Jesus came. So the other disciples said to him, "We have seen the Lord." But he said to them, "Unless I see the mark of the nails in his hands and put my finger into the nailmarks and put my hand into his side, I will not believe."

Now a week later his disciples were again inside and Thomas was with them. Jesus came, although the doors were locked, and stood in their midst and said, "Peace be with you." Then he said to Thomas, "Put your finger here and see my hands, and bring your hand and put it into my side, and do not be unbelieving, but believe." Thomas answered and said to him, "My Lord and my God!" Jesus said to him, "Have you come to believe because you have seen me? Blessed are those who have not seen and have believed."

Now Jesus did many other signs in the presence of his disciples that are not written in this book. But these are written that you may come to believe that Jesus is the Christ, the Son of God, and that through this belief you may have life in his name.

Meditation (*Meditatio*)

After the reading, take some time to reflect in silence on one or more of the following questions:

- What word or words in this passage caught your attention?
- What in this passage comforted you?
- What in this passage challenged you?

If practicing lectio divina as a family or in a group, after the reflection time, invite the participants to share their responses.

Prayer (*Oratio*)

Read the scripture passage one more time. Bring to the Lord the praise, petition, or thanksgiving that the Word inspires in you.

Contemplation (*Contemplatio*)

Read the Scripture again, followed by this reflection:

≈ What conversion of mind, heart, and life is the Lord asking of me?

_____

_____

_____

_____

~ *When the doors were locked . . . for fear.* What fears prevent me from sharing my faith? What fears keep me from reaching out to others in love?

_____

_____

_____

_____

~ *He showed them his hands and his side.* When have I seen Jesus in my suffering brothers and sisters? What suffering can I offer for the needs of the world?

_____

_____

_____

_____

~ *Blessed are those who have not seen and have believed.* What people or events helped me to grow in faith? How can I share Christ with those who do not believe?

_____

_____

_____

_____

∾ After a period of silent reflection and/or discussion, all recite the Lord's Prayer and the following:

Closing Prayer

Let the house of Israel say,
    "His mercy endures forever."
Let the house of Aaron say,
    "His mercy endures forever."
Let those who fear the LORD say,
    "His mercy endures forever."

I was hard pressed and was falling,
    but the LORD helped me.
My strength and my courage is the LORD,
    and he has been my savior.
The joyful shout of victory
    in the tents of the just:

The stone which the builders rejected
    has become the cornerstone.
By the LORD has this been done;
    it is wonderful in our eyes.
This is the day the LORD has made;
    let us be glad and rejoice in it.

From Psalm 118

Living the Word This Week

How can I make my life a gift for others in charity?

Look for ways to participate in your parish or diocesan evangelization efforts.

May 1, 2022

Lectio Divina for the Third Week of Easter

We begin our prayer:

In the name of the Father, and of the Son, and of the Holy Spirit. Amen.

O God, who in the font of Baptism
have made new those who believe in you,
keep safe those reborn in Christ,
that, defeating every onslaught of error,
they may faithfully preserve the grace of your blessing.
Through our Lord Jesus Christ, your Son,
who lives and reigns with you in the unity of the Holy Spirit,
God, for ever and ever.

Collect, Saturday of the Third Week of Easter

Reading (*Lectio*)

Read the following Scripture two or three times.

John 21:1-19 or 21:1-14

At that time, Jesus revealed himself again to his disciples at the Sea of Tiberias. He revealed himself in this way. Together were Simon Peter, Thomas called Didymus, Nathanael from Cana in Galilee, Zebedee's sons, and two others of his disciples. Simon Peter said to them, "I am going fishing." They said to him, "We also will come with you." So they went out and got into the boat, but that night they caught nothing. When it was already dawn, Jesus was standing on the shore; but the disciples did not realize that it was Jesus. Jesus said to them, "Children, have you caught anything to eat?" They answered him, "No." So he said to them, "Cast the net over the right side of the boat and you will find something." So they cast it, and were not able to pull it in because of the number of fish. So the disciple whom Jesus loved said to Peter, "It is the Lord." When Simon Peter heard that it was the Lord, he tucked in his garment, for he was lightly clad, and jumped into the sea. The other disciples came in the boat, for they were not far from shore, only about a hundred yards, dragging the net with the fish. When they climbed out on shore, they saw a charcoal fire with fish on it and bread. Jesus said to them, "Bring some of the fish you just caught." So Simon Peter went over and dragged the net ashore full of one hundred fifty-three large fish. Even though there were so many, the net was not torn. Jesus said to them, "Come, have breakfast." And none of the disciples dared to ask him, "Who are you?" because they realized it was the Lord. Jesus came over and took the bread and gave it to them, and in like manner the fish. This was now the third time Jesus was revealed to his disciples after being raised from the dead.

When they had finished breakfast, Jesus said to Simon Peter, "Simon, son of John, do you love me more than these?" Simon Peter answered him, "Yes, Lord, you know that I love you." Jesus said to him, "Feed my lambs." He then said to Simon Peter a second time, "Simon, son of John, do you love me?" Simon Peter answered him, "Yes, Lord, you know that I love you." Jesus said to him, "Tend my sheep." Jesus said to him the third time, "Simon, son of John, do you love me?" Peter was distressed that Jesus had said to him a third time, "Do you love me?" and he said to him, "Lord, you know everything; you know that I love you." Jesus said to him, "Feed my sheep. Amen, amen, I say to you, when you were younger, you used to dress yourself and go where you wanted; but when you grow old, you will stretch out your hands, and someone else will dress you and lead you where you do not want to go." He said this signifying by what kind of death he would glorify God. And when he had said this, he said to him, "Follow me."

Meditation (*Meditatio*)

After the reading, take some time to reflect in silence on one or more of the following questions:

- What word or words in this passage caught your attention?
- What in this passage comforted you?
- What in this passage challenged you?

If practicing lectio divina as a family or in a group, after the reflection time, invite the participants to share their responses.

Prayer (*Oratio*)

Read the scripture passage one more time. Bring to the Lord the praise, petition, or thanksgiving that the Word inspires in you.

Contemplation (*Contemplatio*)

Read the Scripture again, followed by this reflection:

≈ What conversion of mind, heart, and life is the Lord asking of me?

_____

_____

_____

_____

≈ *So they went out and got into the boat, but that night they caught nothing.* When have I felt as though my spiritual practice is fruitless? What helps me to persevere in living my faith?

_____

_____

_____

_____

~ *So the disciple whom Jesus loved said to Peter, "It is the Lord."* Who has helped me to recognize the Lord? How can I help others to encounter Jesus?

_____

_____

_____

_____

~ *Lord, you know everything; you know that I love you.* How do I show my love for God? How do I feel God's love for me?

_____

_____

_____

_____

~ *After a period of silent reflection and/or discussion, all recite the Lord's Prayer and the following:*

Closing Prayer

I will extol you, O Lord, for you drew me clear
    and did not let my enemies rejoice over me.
O Lord, you brought me up from the netherworld;
    you preserved me from among those going down into the pit.

Sing praise to the LORD, you his faithful ones,
　　and give thanks to his holy name.
For his anger lasts but a moment;
　　a lifetime, his good will.
At nightfall, weeping enters in,
　　but with the dawn, rejoicing.

Hear, O LORD, and have pity on me;
　　O LORD, be my helper.
You changed my mourning into dancing;
　　O LORD, my God, forever will I give you thanks.

From Psalm 30

Living the Word This Week

How can I make my life a gift for others in charity?

Spend some time praying before the Blessed Sacrament, resting in God's love.

May 8, 2022

Lectio Divina for the Fourth Week of Easter

We begin our prayer:

In the name of the Father, and of the Son, and of the Holy Spirit. Amen.

O God, author of our freedom and of our salvation,
listen to the voice of our pleading
and grant that those you have redeemed
by the shedding of your Son's Blood
may have life through you
and, under your protection,
rejoice for ever unharmed.
Through our Lord Jesus Christ, your Son,
who lives and reigns with you in the unity of the Holy Spirit,
God, for ever and ever.

Collect, Friday of the Fourth Week of Easter

Reading (*Lectio*)

Read the following Scripture two or three times.

John 10:27-30

> Jesus said: "My sheep hear my voice; I know them, and they follow me. I give them eternal life, and they shall never perish. No one can take them out of my hand. My Father, who has given them to me, is greater than all, and no one can take them out of the Father's hand. The Father and I are one."

Meditation (*Meditatio*)

After the reading, take some time to reflect in silence on one or more of the following questions:

- What word or words in this passage caught your attention?
- What in this passage comforted you?
- What in this passage challenged you?

If practicing lectio divina as a family or in a group, after the reflection time, invite the participants to share their responses.

Prayer (*Oratio*)

Read the scripture passage one more time. Bring to the Lord the praise, petition, or thanksgiving that the Word inspires in you.

Contemplation (*Contemplatio*)

Read the Scripture again, followed by this reflection:

∾ What conversion of mind, heart, and life is the Lord asking of me?

_____

_____

_____

_____

∾ *I know them.* What parts of my heart do I try to hide from God? How can I strive to know God as God knows me?

_____

_____

_____

_____

∾ *No one can take them out of my hand.* When have I felt God's protective care? How can I support those who struggle in their faith?

_____

_____

~ *My Father, who has given them to me, is greater than all.* When have I seen God's power in action? How can I nurture a sense of wonder and awe in God's presence?

_____

_____

_____

_____

~ *After a period of silent reflection and/or discussion, all recite the Lord's Prayer and the following:*

Closing Prayer

Sing joyfully to the LORD, all you lands;
   serve the LORD with gladness;
   come before him with joyful song.

Know that the LORD is God;
   he made us, his we are;
   his people, the flock he tends.

The LORD is good:
  his kindness endures forever,
  and his faithfulness, to all generations.

From Psalm 100

Living the Word This Week

How can I make my life a gift for others in charity?

Find a way to support the pro-life efforts in your parish to walk with moms in need.

May 15, 2022

Lectio Divina for the Fifth Week of Easter

We begin our prayer:

In the name of the Father, and of the Son, and of the Holy Spirit. Amen.

O God, restorer and lover of innocence,
direct the hearts of your servants towards yourself,
that those you have set free from the darkness of unbelief
may never stray from the light of your truth.
Through our Lord Jesus Christ, your Son,
who lives and reigns with you in the unity of the Holy Spirit,
God, for ever and ever.

Collect, Wednesday of the Fifth Week of Easter

Reading (*Lectio*)

Read the following Scripture two or three times.

John 13:31-33a, 34-35

When Judas had left them, Jesus said, "Now is the Son of Man glorified, and God is glorified in him. If God is glorified in him, God will also glorify him in himself, and God will glorify him at once. My children, I will be with you only a little while longer. I give you a new commandment: love one another. As I have loved you, so you also should love one another. This is how all will know that you are my disciples, if you have love for one another."

Meditation (*Meditatio*)

After the reading, take some time to reflect in silence on one or more of the following questions:

- What word or words in this passage caught your attention?
- What in this passage comforted you?
- What in this passage challenged you?

If practicing lectio divina as a family or in a group, after the reflection time, invite the participants to share their responses.

Prayer (*Oratio*)

Read the scripture passage one more time. Bring to the Lord the praise, petition, or thanksgiving that the Word inspires in you.

Contemplation (*Contemplatio*)

Read the Scripture again, followed by this reflection:

≈ What conversion of mind, heart, and life is the Lord asking of me?

_____

_____

〜 *My children, I will be with you only a little while longer.* When have I felt that God is far away from me? When have I felt that God is near?

_____

_____

_____

_____

〜 *I give you a new commandment: love one another.* Who is most in need of my love this week? Who is it challenging for me to love?

_____

_____

_____

_____

〜 *This is how all will know that you are my disciples, if you have love for one another.* How do I respond to others in faith? How can I put my faith in action more effectively?

_____

_____

∾ *After a period of silent reflection and/or discussion, all recite the Lord's Prayer and the following:*

Closing Prayer

The LORD is gracious and merciful,
    slow to anger and of great kindness.
The LORD is good to all
    and compassionate toward all his works.

Let all your works give you thanks, O LORD,
    and let your faithful ones bless you.
Let them discourse of the glory of your kingdom
    and speak of your might.

Let them make known your might to the children of Adam,
    and the glorious splendor of your kingdom.
Your kingdom is a kingdom for all ages,
    and your dominion endures through all generations.

From Psalm 145

Living the Word This Week

How can I make my life a gift for others in charity?

Learn more about Catholic social teaching (*www.usccb.org/offices/justice -peace-human-development/catholic-social-teaching*) as a way to put your faith into practice.

May 22, 2022

Lectio Divina for the Sixth Week of Easter

We begin our prayer:

In the name of the Father, and of the Son, and of the Holy Spirit. Amen.

Grant, O merciful God,
that we may experience at all times
the fruit produced by the paschal observances.
Through our Lord Jesus Christ, your Son,
who lives and reigns with you in the unity of the Holy Spirit,
God, for ever and ever.

Collect, Monday of the Sixth Week of Easter

Reading (*Lectio*)

Read the following Scripture two or three times.

John 14:23-29

> Jesus said to his disciples: "Whoever loves me will keep my word,
> and my Father will love him, and we will come to him and make
> our dwelling with him. Whoever does not love me does not keep

my words; yet the word you hear is not mine but that of the Father who sent me.

"I have told you this while I am with you. The Advocate, the Holy Spirit, whom the Father will send in my name, will teach you everything and remind you of all that I told you. Peace I leave with you; my peace I give to you. Not as the world gives do I give it to you. Do not let your hearts be troubled or afraid. You heard me tell you, 'I am going away and I will come back to you.' If you loved me, you would rejoice that I am going to the Father; for the Father is greater than I. And now I have told you this before it happens, so that when it happens you may believe."

Meditation (*Meditatio*)

After the reading, take some time to reflect in silence on one or more of the following questions:

- What word or words in this passage caught your attention?
- What in this passage comforted you?
- What in this passage challenged you?

If practicing lectio divina as a family or in a group, after the reflection time, invite the participants to share their responses.

Prayer (*Oratio*)

Read the scripture passage one more time. Bring to the Lord the praise, petition, or thanksgiving that the Word inspires in you.

Contemplation (*Contemplatio*)

Read the Scripture again, followed by this reflection:

∼ What conversion of mind, heart, and life is the Lord asking of me?

_____

_____

_____

_____

∼ *We will come to him and make our dwelling with him.* Where do I feel the presence of God most strongly? How can I encounter the Lord dwelling in others?

_____

_____

_____

_____

∼ *The Advocate, the Holy Spirit, whom the Father will send in my name, will teach you everything.* How well do I know my faith? How can I grow in my knowledge and love of God?

_____

_____

_____

_____

~ *Not as the world gives* [*peace*] *do I give it to you.* In what parts of my life do I feel a need for God's peace? How can I be a force for peace and unity?

_____

_____

_____

_____

~ *After a period of silent reflection and/or discussion, all recite the Lord's Prayer and the following:*

Closing Prayer

May God have pity on us and bless us;
    may he let his face shine upon us.
So may your way be known upon earth;
    among all nations, your salvation.

May the nations be glad and exult
    because you rule the peoples in equity;
    the nations on the earth you guide.

May the peoples praise you, O God;
    may all the peoples praise you!
May God bless us,
    and may all the ends of the earth fear him!

From Psalm 67

Living the Word This Week

How can I make my life a gift for others in charity?

Read chapter 7 of Pope Francis's encyclical *Fratelli Tutti* on peace and forgiveness (*www.vatican.va/content/francesco/en/encyclicals/ documents/papa-francesco_20201003_enciclica-fratelli-tutti.html*).

May 26, 2022

Lectio Divina for the Solemnity of the Ascension

We begin our prayer:

In the name of the Father, and of the Son, and of the Holy Spirit. Amen.

Gladden us with holy joys, almighty God,
and make us rejoice with devout thanksgiving,
for the Ascension of Christ your Son
is our exaltation,
and, where the Head has gone before in glory,
the Body is called to follow in hope.
Through our Lord Jesus Christ, your Son,
who lives and reigns with you in the unity of the Holy Spirit,
God, for ever and ever.

Collect, Ascension, Mass during the Day

Reading (*Lectio*)

Read the following Scripture two or three times.

Luke 24:46-53

Jesus said to his disciples: "Thus it is written that the Christ would suffer and rise from the dead on the third day and that repentance, for the forgiveness of sins, would be preached in his name to all the nations, beginning from Jerusalem. You are witnesses of these things. And behold I am sending the promise of my Father upon you; but stay in the city until you are clothed with power from on high."

Then he led them out as far as Bethany, raised his hands, and blessed them. As he blessed them he parted from them and was taken up to heaven. They did him homage and then returned to Jerusalem with great joy, and they were continually in the temple praising God.

Meditation (*Meditatio*)

After the reading, take some time to reflect in silence on one or more of the following questions:

- What word or words in this passage caught your attention?
- What in this passage comforted you?
- What in this passage challenged you?

If practicing lectio divina as a family or in a group, after the reflection time, invite the participants to share their responses.

Prayer (*Oratio*)

Read the scripture passage one more time. Bring to the Lord the praise, petition, or thanksgiving that the Word inspires in you.

Contemplation (*Contemplatio*)

Read the Scripture again, followed by this reflection:

≈ What conversion of mind, heart, and life is the Lord asking of me?

_____

_____

_____

_____

≈ *Thus it is written that the Christ would suffer.* What hardships am I facing? How can I unite my suffering to the suffering of Christ?

_____

_____

_____

_____

≈ *I am sending the promise of my Father upon you.* On what promises of God do I most rely? How can I increase in my trust of God's promises?

_____

_____

_____

_____

≈ *They did him homage and then returned to Jerusalem with great joy.* What about my faith brings me joy? How can I share that joy with others?

_____

_____

_____

_____

≈ *After a period of silent reflection and/or discussion, all recite the Lord's Prayer and the following:*

Closing Prayer

All you peoples, clap your hands,
   shout to God with cries of gladness,
For the LORD, the Most High, the awesome,
   is the great king over all the earth.

God mounts his throne amid shouts of joy;
>   the LORD, amid trumpet blasts.
Sing praise to God, sing praise;
>   sing praise to our king, sing praise.

For king of all the earth is God;
>   sing hymns of praise.
God reigns over the nations,
>   God sits upon his holy throne.

From Psalm 47

Living the Word This Week

How can I make my life a gift for others in charity?

Offer up a hardship or other challenge for the intentions of the Church and the world.

May 29, 2022

Lectio Divina for the Seventh Week of Easter

We begin our prayer:

In the name of the Father, and of the Son, and of the Holy Spirit. Amen.

Grant, we pray, almighty and merciful God,
that the Holy Spirit, coming near
and dwelling graciously within us,
may make of us a perfect temple of his glory.
Through our Lord Jesus Christ, your Son,
who lives and reigns with you in the unity of the Holy Spirit,
God, for ever and ever.

Collect, Tuesday of the Seventh Week of Easter

Reading (*Lectio*)

Read the following Scripture two or three times.

John 17:20-26

> Lifting up his eyes to heaven, Jesus prayed saying: "Holy Father, I pray not only for them, but also for those who will believe in me through their word, so that they may all be one, as you, Father, are in me and I in you, that they also may be in us, that the world may believe that you sent me. And I have given them the glory you gave me, so that they may be one, as we are one, I in them and you in me, that they may be brought to perfection as one, that the world may know that you sent me, and that you loved them even as you loved me. Father, they are your gift to me. I wish that where I am they also may be with me, that they may see my glory that you gave me, because you loved me before the foundation of the world. Righteous Father, the world also does not know you, but I know you, and they know that you sent me. I made known to them your name and I will make it known, that the love with which you loved me may be in them and I in them."

Meditation (*Meditatio*)

After the reading, take some time to reflect in silence on one or more of the following questions:

- What word or words in this passage caught your attention?
- What in this passage comforted you?
- What in this passage challenged you?

If practicing lectio divina as a family or in a group, after the reflection time, invite the participants to share their responses.

Prayer (*Oratio*)

Read the scripture passage one more time. Bring to the Lord the praise, petition, or thanksgiving that the Word inspires in you.

Contemplation (*Contemplatio*)

Read the Scripture again, followed by this reflection:

∾ What conversion of mind, heart, and life is the Lord asking of me?

_____

_____

_____

_____

∾ *That the world may believe that you sent me.* How often do I encounter those who do not believe in God or who have abandoned the practice of their faith? How can I offer welcome and support to those people?

_____

_____

_____

_____

≈ *That they may be brought to perfection as one.* What parts of my life need perfecting? How can I nurture a spirit of continuing conversion?

_____

_____

_____

_____

≈ *That where I am they also may be with me.* How can I remind myself of God's presence and action in my life? How can I follow Jesus more closely?

_____

_____

_____

_____

≈ *After a period of silent reflection and/or discussion, all recite the Lord's Prayer and the following:*

Closing Prayer

The LORD is king; let the earth rejoice;
    let the many islands be glad.
Justice and judgment are the foundation of his throne.

The heavens proclaim his justice,
and all peoples see his glory.
All gods are prostrate before him.

You, O LORD, are the Most High over all the earth,
exalted far above all gods.

From Psalm 97

Living the Word This Week

How can I make my life a gift for others in charity?

Learn more about outreach to the religiously unaffiliated: *www.usccb .org/committees/evangelization-catechesis/outreach-unaffiliated.*

June 5, 2022

Lectio Divina for the Solemnity of Pentecost

We begin our prayer:

In the name of the Father, and of the Son, and of the Holy Spirit. Amen.

Grant, we pray, almighty God,
that the splendor of your glory
may shine forth upon us
and that, by the bright rays of the Holy Spirit,
the light of your light may confirm the hearts
of those born again by your grace.
Through our Lord Jesus Christ, your Son,
who lives and reigns with you in the unity of the Holy Spirit,
God, for ever and ever.

Collect, Pentecost, Vigil Mass, second option

Reading (*Lectio*)

Read the following Scripture two or three times.

John 14:15-16, 23b-26

> Jesus said to his disciples: "If you love me, you will keep my commandments. And I will ask the Father, and he will give you another Advocate to be with you always.

> "Whoever loves me will keep my word, and my Father will love him, and we will come to him and make our dwelling with him. Those who do not love me do not keep my words; yet the word you hear is not mine but that of the Father who sent me.

> "I have told you this while I am with you. The Advocate, the Holy Spirit whom the Father will send in my name, will teach you everything and remind you of all that I told you."

Meditation (*Meditatio*)

After the reading, take some time to reflect in silence on one or more of the following questions:

- What word or words in this passage caught your attention?
- What in this passage comforted you?
- What in this passage challenged you?

If practicing lectio divina as a family or in a group, after the reflection time, invite the participants to share their responses.

Prayer (*Oratio*)

Read the scripture passage one more time. Bring to the Lord the praise, petition, or thanksgiving that the Word inspires in you.

Contemplation (*Contemplatio*)

Read the Scripture again, followed by this reflection:

≈ What conversion of mind, heart, and life is the Lord asking of me?

_____

_____

_____

_____

≈ *He will give you another Advocate to be with you always.* How has the gift of the Spirit enriched my life? How can I nurture the fruits of the Spirit in my daily living?

_____

_____

_____

_____

~ *Whoever loves me will keep my word.* How can I make reading and praying with Scripture part of my life? How can Scripture help me to grow in my love for God and for my neighbor?

_____

_____

_____

_____

~ *The word you hear is not mine.* How can I discern the voice of God? What reliable sources can I access to learn about my faith?

_____

_____

_____

_____

~ *After a period of silent reflection and/or discussion, all recite the Lord's Prayer and the following:*

Closing Prayer

Bless the Lord, O my soul!
  O Lord, my God, you are great indeed!
How manifold are your works, O Lord!
  the earth is full of your creatures;

If you take away their breath, they perish
    and return to their dust.
When you send forth your spirit, they are created,
    and you renew the face of the earth.

May the glory of the LORD endure forever;
    may the LORD be glad in his works!
Pleasing to him be my theme;
    I will be glad in the LORD.

From Psalm 104

Living the Word This Week

How can I make my life a gift for others in charity?

Join a diocesan, state, or national advocacy effort to speak out on behalf of the underprivileged and voiceless.

June 12, 2022

Lectio Divina for the Solemnity of the Most Holy Trinity

We begin our prayer:

In the name of the Father, and of the Son, and of the Holy Spirit. Amen.

God our Father, who by sending into the world
the Word of truth and the Spirit of sanctification
made known to the human race your wondrous mystery,
grant us, we pray, that in professing the true faith,
we may acknowledge the Trinity of eternal glory
and adore your Unity, powerful in majesty.
Through our Lord Jesus Christ, your Son,
who lives and reigns with you in the unity of the Holy Spirit,
God, for ever and ever.

Collect, Solemnity of the Most Holy Trinity

Reading (*Lectio*)

Read the following Scripture two or three times.

John 16:12-15

> Jesus said to his disciples: "I have much more to tell you, but you cannot bear it now. But when he comes, the Spirit of truth, he will guide you to all truth. He will not speak on his own, but he will speak what he hears, and will declare to you the things that are coming. He will glorify me, because he will take from what is mine and declare it to you. Everything that the Father has is mine; for this reason I told you that he will take from what is mine and declare it to you."

Meditation (*Meditatio*)

After the reading, take some time to reflect in silence on one or more of the following questions:

- What word or words in this passage caught your attention?
- What in this passage comforted you?
- What in this passage challenged you?

If practicing lectio divina as a family or in a group, after the reflection time, invite the participants to share their responses.

Prayer (*Oratio*)

Read the scripture passage one more time. Bring to the Lord the praise, petition, or thanksgiving that the Word inspires in you.

Contemplation (*Contemplatio*)

Read the Scripture again, followed by this reflection:

≈ What conversion of mind, heart, and life is the Lord asking of me?

_____

_____

_____

_____

≈ *I have much more to tell you.* What areas of Church teaching should I learn more about? How can I learn more about these areas?

_____

_____

_____

_____

≈ *He . . . will declare to you the things that are coming.* What anxieties do I have about the future? What obstacles keep me from being a prophetic voice?

_____

_____

_____

_____

� *He will take from what is mine and declare it to you.* How do I show respect and submission to the Church's deposit of faith? How do I share that deposit of faith with others?

_____

_____

_____

_____

� *After a period of silent reflection and/or discussion, all recite the Lord's Prayer and the following:*

Closing Prayer

When I behold your heavens, the work of your fingers,
  the moon and the stars which you set in place—
What is man that you should be mindful of him,
  or the son of man that you should care for him?

You have made him little less than the angels,
  and crowned him with glory and honor.
You have given him rule over the works of your hands,
  putting all things under his feet:

All sheep and oxen,
    yes, and the beasts of the field,
The birds of the air, the fishes of the sea,
    and whatever swims the paths of the seas.

From Psalm 8

Living the Word This Week

How can I make my life a gift for others in charity?

Research your parish's catechetical efforts and consider participating as a catechist, sponsor, or learner.

June 19, 2022

Lectio Divina for the Solemnity of the Most Holy Body and Blood of Christ (*Corpus Christi*)

We begin our prayer:

In the name of the Father, and of the Son, and of the Holy Spirit. Amen.

O God, who in this wonderful Sacrament
have left us a memorial of your Passion,
grant us, we pray,
so to revere the sacred mysteries of your Body and Blood
that we may always experience in ourselves
the fruits of your redemption.
Who live and reign with God the Father
in the unity of the Holy Spirit,
God, for ever and ever.

Collect, Solemnity of the Most Holy Body and Blood of Christ

Reading (*Lectio*)

Read the following Scripture two or three times.

Luke 9:11b-17

> Jesus spoke to the crowds about the kingdom of God, and he healed those who needed to be cured. As the day was drawing to a close, the Twelve approached him and said, "Dismiss the crowd so that they can go to the surrounding villages and farms and find lodging and provisions; for we are in a deserted place here." He said to them, "Give them some food yourselves." They replied, "Five loaves and two fish are all we have, unless we ourselves go and buy food for all these people." Now the men there numbered about five thousand. Then he said to his disciples, "Have them sit down in groups of about fifty." They did so and made them all sit down. Then taking the five loaves and the two fish, and looking up to heaven, he said the blessing over them, broke them, and gave them to the disciples to set before the crowd. They all ate and were satisfied. And when the leftover fragments were picked up, they filled twelve wicker baskets.

Meditation (*Meditatio*)

After the reading, take some time to reflect in silence on one or more of the following questions:

- What word or words in this passage caught your attention?
- What in this passage comforted you?
- What in this passage challenged you?

If practicing lectio divina as a family or in a group, after the reflection time, invite the participants to share their responses.

Prayer (*Oratio*)

Read the scripture passage one more time. Bring to the Lord the praise, petition, or thanksgiving that the Word inspires in you.

Contemplation (*Contemplatio*)

Read the Scripture again, followed by this reflection:

∼ What conversion of mind, heart, and life is the Lord asking of me?

_____

_____

_____

_____

∼ *Jesus spoke to the crowds about the kingdom of God.* How do I imagine the kingdom of God? How do I see the inbreaking of the kingdom in this world?

_____

_____

_____

_____

～ *We are in a deserted place here.* When have I felt alone and abandoned by God? How can I become more aware of God's presence?

_____

_____

_____

_____

～ *And when the leftover fragments were picked up, they filled twelve wicker baskets.* In what ways do I waste God's gifts? How can I respond with gratitude to God's generosity?

_____

_____

_____

_____

～ *After a period of silent reflection and/or discussion, all recite the Lord's Prayer and the following:*

Closing Prayer

The LORD said to my Lord: "Sit at my right hand
   till I make your enemies your footstool."

The scepter of your power the LORD will stretch forth from Zion:
   "Rule in the midst of your enemies."

"Yours is princely power in the day of your birth, in holy splendor;
before the daystar, like the dew, I have begotten you."

The LORD has sworn, and he will not repent:
"You are a priest forever, according to the order of Melchizedek."

From Psalm 110

Living the Word This Week

How can I make my life a gift for others in charity?

Make a contribution in cash or in kind to your parish food pantry or
to a local food bank.

June 24, 2022

Lectio Divina for the Solemnity of the Sacred Heart

We begin our prayer:

In the name of the Father, and of the Son, and of the Holy Spirit. Amen.

Grant, we pray, almighty God,
that we, who glory in the Heart of your beloved Son
and recall the wonders of his love for us,
may be made worthy to receive
an overflowing measure of grace
from that fount of heavenly gifts.
Through our Lord Jesus Christ, your Son,
who lives and reigns with you in the unity of the Holy Spirit,
God, for ever and ever.

Collect, Solemnity of the Sacred Heart, first option

Reading (*Lectio*)

Read the following Scripture two or three times.

Luke 15:3-7

> Jesus addressed this parable to the Pharisees and scribes: "What man among you having a hundred sheep and losing one of them would not leave the ninety-nine in the desert and go after the lost one until he finds it? And when he does find it, he sets it on his shoulders with great joy and, upon his arrival home, he calls together his friends and neighbors and says to them, 'Rejoice with me because I have found my lost sheep.' I tell you, in just the same way there will be more joy in heaven over one sinner who repents than over ninety-nine righteous people who have no need of repentance."

Meditation (*Meditatio*)

After the reading, take some time to reflect in silence on one or more of the following questions:

- What word or words in this passage caught your attention?
- What in this passage comforted you?
- What in this passage challenged you?

If practicing lectio divina as a family or in a group, after the reflection time, invite the participants to share their responses.

Prayer (*Oratio*)

Read the scripture passage one more time. Bring to the Lord the praise, petition, or thanksgiving that the Word inspires in you.

Contemplation (*Contemplatio*)

Read the Scripture again, followed by this reflection:

~ What conversion of mind, heart, and life is the Lord asking of me?

\
\
\
\

~ *What man among you having a hundred sheep and losing one of them would not leave the ninety-nine in the desert and go after the lost one until he finds it?* How do I keep holy the Lord's day? How can my faith be solemn and joy-filled?

\
\
\
\

~ *Rejoice with me because I have found my lost sheep.* Whose testimony has helped me come to know God more fully? How can I discern what is true?

_____

_____

_____

_____

~ *There will be more joy in heaven over one sinner who repents than over ninety-nine righteous people who have no need of repentance.* How have my sins added to Jesus' burden? How can I bear my cross more patiently?

_____

_____

_____

_____

~ *After a period of silent reflection and/or discussion, all recite the Lord's Prayer and the following:*

Closing Prayer

The LORD is my shepherd; I shall not want.
  In verdant pastures he gives me repose;
beside restful waters he leads me;
  he refreshes my soul.

He guides me in right paths
  for his name's sake.
Even though I walk in the dark valley
  I fear no evil; for you are at my side
with your rod and your staff
  that give me courage.

You spread the table before me
  in the sight of my foes;
you anoint my head with oil;
  my cup overflows.

Only goodness and kindness follow me
  all the days of my life;
and I shall dwell in the house of the LORD
  for years to come.

From Psalm 23

Living the Word This Week

How can I make my life a gift for others in charity?

Pray a Rosary of Healing and Protection (*www.usccb.org/issues-and-action/child-and-youth-protection/upload/Rosary-for-Healing-Printable.pdf*).

June 26, 2022

Lectio Divina for the Thirteenth Week in Ordinary Time

We begin our prayer:

In the name of the Father, and of the Son, and of the Holy Spirit. Amen.

O God, who through the grace of adoption
chose us to be children of light,
grant, we pray,
that we may not be wrapped in the darkness of error
but always be seen to stand in the bright light of truth.
Through our Lord Jesus Christ, your Son,
who lives and reigns with you in the unity of the Holy Spirit,
God, for ever and ever.

Collect, Thirteenth Sunday in Ordinary Time

Reading (*Lectio*)

Read the following Scripture two or three times.

Luke 9:51-62

When the days for Jesus' being taken up were fulfilled, he resolutely determined to journey to Jerusalem, and he sent messengers ahead of him. On the way they entered a Samaritan village to prepare for his reception there, but they would not welcome him because the destination of his journey was Jerusalem. When the disciples James and John saw this they asked, "Lord, do you want us to call down fire from heaven to consume them?" Jesus turned and rebuked them, and they journeyed to another village.

As they were proceeding on their journey someone said to him, "I will follow you wherever you go." Jesus answered him, "Foxes have dens and birds of the sky have nests, but the Son of Man has nowhere to rest his head."

And to another he said, "Follow me." But he replied, "Lord, let me go first and bury my father." But he answered him, "Let the dead bury their dead. But you, go and proclaim the kingdom of God." And another said, "I will follow you, Lord, but first let me say farewell to my family at home." To him Jesus said, "No one who sets a hand to the plow and looks to what was left behind is fit for the kingdom of God."

Meditation (*Meditatio*)

After the reading, take some time to reflect in silence on one or more of the following questions:

- What word or words in this passage caught your attention?
- What in this passage comforted you?
- What in this passage challenged you?

If practicing lectio divina as a family or in a group, after the reflection time, invite the participants to share their responses.

Prayer (*Oratio*)

Read the scripture passage one more time. Bring to the Lord the praise, petition, or thanksgiving that the Word inspires in you.

Contemplation (*Contemplatio*)

Read the Scripture again, followed by this reflection:

∿ What conversion of mind, heart, and life is the Lord asking of me?

~ *He resolutely determined to journey to Jerusalem.* Where is God calling me to go? How resolute am I in my faith journey?

_____

_____

_____

_____

~ *The Son of Man has nowhere to rest his head.* Do I take time to rest and refresh myself? How can I be more hospitable and welcoming to others?

_____

_____

_____

_____

~ *But you, go and proclaim the kingdom of God.* How can I proclaim the kingdom of God more effectively? How can my life more fully reflect my beliefs?

_____

_____

_____

_____

After a period of silent reflection and/or discussion, all recite the Lord's Prayer and the following:

Closing Prayer

Keep me, O God, for in you I take refuge;
>   I say to the LORD, "My Lord are you.
O LORD, my allotted portion and my cup,
>   you it is who hold fast my lot."

I bless the LORD who counsels me;
>   even in the night my heart exhorts me.
I set the LORD ever before me;
>   with him at my right hand I shall not be disturbed.

Therefore my heart is glad and my soul rejoices,
>   my body, too, abides in confidence
because you will not abandon my soul to the netherworld,
>   nor will you suffer your faithful one to undergo corruption.

You will show me the path to life,
>   fullness of joys in your presence,
>   the delights at your right hand forever.

From Psalm 16

Living the Word This Week

How can I make my life a gift for others in charity?

Pray for those who have been recently ordained to the priesthood or diaconate, those who have recently professed religious vows, and those who are discerning their vocation.

June 29, 2022

Lectio Divina for the Solemnity of Saints Peter and Paul

We begin our prayer:

In the name of the Father, and of the Son, and of the Holy Spirit. Amen.

Grant, we pray, O Lord our God,
that we may be sustained
by the intercession of the blessed Apostles Peter and Paul,
that, as through them you gave your Church
the foundations of her heavenly office,
so through them you may help her to eternal salvation.
Through our Lord Jesus Christ, your Son,
who lives and reigns with you in the unity of the Holy Spirit,
God, for ever and ever.

Collect, Solemnity of Saints Peter and Paul, Vigil Mass

Reading (*Lectio*)

Read the following Scripture two or three times.

Matthew 16:13-19

> When Jesus went into the region of Caesarea Philippi he asked his disciples, "Who do people say that the Son of Man is?" They replied, "Some say John the Baptist, others Elijah, still others Jeremiah or one of the prophets." He said to them, "But who do you say that I am?" Simon Peter said in reply, "You are the Christ, the Son of the living God." Jesus said to him in reply, "Blessed are you, Simon son of Jonah. For flesh and blood has not revealed this to you, but my heavenly Father. And so I say to you, you are Peter, and upon this rock I will build my Church, and the gates of the netherworld shall not prevail against it. I will give you the keys to the Kingdom of heaven. Whatever you bind on earth shall be bound in heaven; and whatever you loose on earth shall be loosed in heaven."

Meditation (*Meditatio*)

After the reading, take some time to reflect in silence on one or more of the following questions:

- What word or words in this passage caught your attention?
- What in this passage comforted you?
- What in this passage challenged you?

If practicing lectio divina as a family or in a group, after the reflection time, invite the participants to share their responses.

Prayer (*Oratio*)

Read the scripture passage one more time. Bring to the Lord the praise, petition, or thanksgiving that the Word inspires in you.

Contemplation (*Contemplatio*)

Read the Scripture again, followed by this reflection:

∼ What conversion of mind, heart, and life is the Lord asking of me?

_____

_____

_____

_____

∼ *You are the Christ, the Son of the living God.* How have I encountered Christ this week? How do my actions testify to my faith in Christ?

_____

_____

_____

_____

~ *For flesh and blood has not revealed this to you, but my heavenly Father.* Who has helped me come to know God? How has God revealed himself to me?

_____

_____

_____

_____

~ *Whatever you bind on earth shall be bound in heaven; and whatever you loose on earth shall be loosed in heaven.* What things bind me to my sinful ways? How can I loosen these bindings?

_____

_____

_____

_____

~ *After a period of silent reflection and/or discussion, all recite the Lord's Prayer and the following:*

Closing Prayer

I will bless the LORD at all times;
    his praise shall be ever in my mouth.
Let my soul glory in the LORD;
    the lowly will hear me and be glad.

Glorify the LORD with me,
  let us together extol his name.
I sought the LORD, and he answered me
  and delivered me from all my fears.

Look to him that you may be radiant with joy,
  and your faces may not blush with shame.
When the poor one called out, the LORD heard,
  and from all his distress he saved him.

The angel of the LORD encamps
  around those who fear him, and delivers them.
Taste and see how good the LORD is;
  blessed the man who takes refuge in him.

From Psalm 34

Living the Word This Week

How can I make my life a gift for others in charity?

Make a good examination of conscience and receive the Sacrament of Penance.

July 3, 2022

Lectio Divina for the Fourteenth Week in Ordinary Time

We begin our prayer:

In the name of the Father, and of the Son, and of the Holy Spirit. Amen.

O God, who in the abasement of your Son
have raised up a fallen world,
fill your faithful with holy joy,
for on those you have rescued from slavery to sin
you bestow eternal gladness.
Through our Lord Jesus Christ, your Son,
who lives and reigns with you in the unity of the Holy Spirit,
God, for ever and ever.

Collect, Fourteenth Sunday in Ordinary Time

Reading (*Lectio*)

Read the following Scripture two or three times.

Luke 10:1-12, 17-20 or 10:1-9

At that time the Lord appointed seventy-two others whom he sent ahead of him in pairs to every town and place he intended to visit. He said to them, "The harvest is abundant but the laborers are few; so ask the master of the harvest to send out laborers for his harvest. Go on your way; behold, I am sending you like lambs among wolves. Carry no money bag, no sack, no sandals; and greet no one along the way. Into whatever house you enter, first say, 'Peace to this household.' If a peaceful person lives there, your peace will rest on him; but if not, it will return to you. Stay in the same house and eat and drink what is offered to you, for the laborer deserves his payment. Do not move about from one house to another. Whatever town you enter and they welcome you, eat what is set before you, cure the sick in it and say to them, 'The kingdom of God is at hand for you.' Whatever town you enter and they do not receive you, go out into the streets and say, 'The dust of your town that clings to our feet, even that we shake off against you.' Yet know this: the kingdom of God is at hand. I tell you, it will be more tolerable for Sodom on that day than for that town."

The seventy-two returned rejoicing, and said, "Lord, even the demons are subject to us because of your name." Jesus said, "I have observed Satan fall like lightning from the sky. Behold, I have given you the power to 'tread upon serpents' and scorpions and upon the full force of the enemy and nothing will harm you. Nevertheless, do not rejoice because the spirits are subject to you, but rejoice because your names are written in heaven."

Meditation (*Meditatio*)

After the reading, take some time to reflect in silence on one or more of the following questions:

- What word or words in this passage caught your attention?
- What in this passage comforted you?
- What in this passage challenged you?

If practicing lectio divina as a family or in a group, after the reflection time, invite the participants to share their responses.

Prayer (*Oratio*)

Read the scripture passage one more time. Bring to the Lord the praise, petition, or thanksgiving that the Word inspires in you.

Contemplation (*Contemplatio*)

Read the Scripture again, followed by this reflection:

∼ What conversion of mind, heart, and life is the Lord asking of me?

_____

_____

_____

_____

~ *Behold, I am sending you like lambs among wolves.* When have I felt that my faith is challenged? What "wolves" do I need to avoid?

_____

_____

_____

_____

~ *Carry no money bag, no sack, no sandals.* When have I placed more faith in my possessions than in God? How can I increase my detachment from worldly goods?

_____

_____

_____

_____

~ *I have given you the power to "tread upon serpents" and scorpions and upon the full force of the enemy and nothing will harm you.* What spiritual practices can strengthen my ability to avoid evil? How can I be a force for good in the world?

_____

_____

After a period of silent reflection and/or discussion, all recite the Lord's Prayer and the following:

Closing Prayer

Shout joyfully to God, all the earth,
　　sing praise to the glory of his name;
　　proclaim his glorious praise.
Say to God, "How tremendous are your deeds!"

"Let all on earth worship and sing praise to you,
　　sing praise to your name!"
Come and see the works of God,
　　his tremendous deeds among the children of Adam.

He has changed the sea into dry land;
　　through the river they passed on foot;
　　therefore let us rejoice in him.
He rules by his might forever.

Hear now, all you who fear God, while I declare
　　what he has done for me.
Blessed be God who refused me not
　　my prayer or his kindness!

From Psalm 66

Living the Word This Week

How can I make my life a gift for others in charity?

Consider contributing your time, treasure, or talent to a local agency that aids the poor, such as the St. Vincent de Paul Society or Catholic Charities.

July 10, 2022

Lectio Divina for the Fifteenth Week in Ordinary Time

We begin our prayer:

In the name of the Father, and of the Son, and of the Holy Spirit. Amen.

O God, who show the light of your truth
to those who go astray,
so that they may return to the right path,
give all who for the faith they profess
are accounted Christians
the grace to reject whatever is contrary to the name of Christ
and to strive after all that does it honor.
Through our Lord Jesus Christ, your Son,
who lives and reigns with you in the unity of the Holy Spirit,
God, for ever and ever.

Collect, Fifteenth Sunday in Ordinary Time

Reading (*Lectio*)

Read the following Scripture two or three times.

Luke 10:25-37

There was a scholar of the law who stood up to test him and said, "Teacher, what must I do to inherit eternal life?" Jesus said to him, "What is written in the law? How do you read it?" He said in reply, *You shall love the Lord, your God, with all your heart, with all your being, with all your strength, and with all your mind, and your neighbor as yourself.*" He replied to him, "You have answered correctly; do this and you will live."

But because he wished to justify himself, he said to Jesus, "And who is my neighbor?" Jesus replied, "A man fell victim to robbers as he went down from Jerusalem to Jericho. They stripped and beat him and went off leaving him half-dead. A priest happened to be going down that road, but when he saw him, he passed by on the opposite side. Likewise a Levite came to the place, and when he saw him, he passed by on the opposite side. But a Samaritan traveler who came upon him was moved with compassion at the sight. He approached the victim, poured oil and wine over his wounds and bandaged them. Then he lifted him up on his own animal, took him to an inn, and cared for him. The next day he took out two silver coins and gave them to the innkeeper with the instruction, 'Take care of him. If you spend more than what I have given you, I shall repay you on my way back.' Which of these three, in your opinion, was neighbor to the robbers' victim?" He answered, "The one who treated him with mercy." Jesus said to him, "Go and do likewise."

Meditation (*Meditatio*)

After the reading, take some time to reflect in silence on one or more of the following questions:

- What word or words in this passage caught your attention?
- What in this passage comforted you?
- What in this passage challenged you?

If practicing lectio divina as a family or in a group, after the reflection time, invite the participants to share their responses.

Prayer (*Oratio*)

Read the scripture passage one more time. Bring to the Lord the praise, petition, or thanksgiving that the Word inspires in you.

Contemplation (*Contemplatio*)

Read the Scripture again, followed by this reflection:

∾ What conversion of mind, heart, and life is the Lord asking of me?

_____

_____

_____

_____

~ *There was a scholar of the law who stood up to test him.* When have I tried to test God? How can I learn to rely more on God's loving providence?

_____

_____

_____

_____

~ *A man fell victim to robbers as he went down from Jerusalem to Jericho.* When have I been hurt or victimized by others? Who has come to my aid?

_____

_____

_____

_____

~ *He passed by on the opposite side.* When have I failed to help those in need? How can I be more attentive to others?

_____

_____

_____

_____

~ *After a period of silent reflection and/or discussion, all recite the Lord's Prayer and the following:*

Closing Prayer

I pray to you, O Lord,
> for the time of your favor, O God!

In your great kindness answer me
> with your constant help.

Answer me, O Lord, for bounteous is your kindness:
> in your great mercy turn toward me.

I am afflicted and in pain;
> let your saving help, O God, protect me.

I will praise the name of God in song,
> and I will glorify him with thanksgiving.

"See, you lowly ones, and be glad;
> you who seek God, may your hearts revive!

For the Lord hears the poor,
> and his own who are in bonds he spurns not."

For God will save Zion
> and rebuild the cities of Judah.

The descendants of his servants shall inherit it,
> and those who love his name shall inhabit it.

From Psalm 69

Living the Word This Week

How can I make my life a gift for others in charity?

Read the reflection on the Parable of the Good Samaritan in Pope Francis's encyclical *Fratelli Tutti* (paragraphs 56-86): *www.vatican.va/content/francesco/en/encyclicals/documents/papa-francesco_20201003_enciclica-fratelli-tutti.html.*

July 17, 2022

Lectio Divina for the Sixteenth Week in Ordinary Time

We begin our prayer:

In the name of the Father, and of the Son, and of the Holy Spirit. Amen.

Show favor, O Lord, to your servants
and mercifully increase the gifts of your grace,
that, made fervent in hope, faith and charity,
they may be ever watchful in keeping your commands.
Through our Lord Jesus Christ, your Son,
who lives and reigns with you in the unity of the Holy Spirit,
God, for ever and ever.

Collect, Sixteenth Sunday in Ordinary Time

Reading (*Lectio*)

Read the following Scripture two or three times.

Luke 10:38-42

> Jesus entered a village where a woman whose name was Martha welcomed him. She had a sister named Mary who sat beside the Lord at his feet listening to him speak. Martha, burdened with much serving, came to him and said, "Lord, do you not care that my sister has left me by myself to do the serving? Tell her to help me." The Lord said to her in reply, "Martha, Martha, you are anxious and worried about many things. There is need of only one thing. Mary has chosen the better part and it will not be taken from her."

Meditation (*Meditatio*)

After the reading, take some time to reflect in silence on one or more of the following questions:

- What word or words in this passage caught your attention?
- What in this passage comforted you?
- What in this passage challenged you?

If practicing lectio divina as a family or in a group, after the reflection time, invite the participants to share their responses.

Prayer (*Oratio*)

Read the scripture passage one more time. Bring to the Lord the praise, petition, or thanksgiving that the Word inspires in you.

Contemplation (*Contemplatio*)

Read the Scripture again, followed by this reflection:

∿ What conversion of mind, heart, and life is the Lord asking of me?

_____

_____

_____

_____

∿ *Mary . . . sat beside the Lord at his feet listening to him speak.* Where do I feel God's presence most profoundly? How can I cultivate a listening heart?

_____

_____

_____

_____

∿ *Burdened with much serving.* What concerns are burdening me at this time? How can I help others bear their burdens?

_____

_____

_____

_____

∾ *Mary has chosen the better part and it will not be taken from her.* What is the better part that I am seeking? How can I prioritize that better part in my life?

_____

_____

_____

_____

∾ *After a period of silent reflection and/or discussion, all recite the Lord's Prayer and the following:*

Closing Prayer

One who walks blamelessly and does justice;
> who thinks the truth in his heart
> and slanders not with his tongue.

Who harms not his fellow man,
> nor takes up a reproach against his neighbor;
by whom the reprobate is despised,
> while he honors those who fear the LORD.

Who lends not his money at usury
 and accepts no bribe against the innocent.
One who does these things
 shall never be disturbed.

From Psalm 15

Living the Word This Week

How can I make my life a gift for others in charity?

Prayerfully consider participation in your parish's ministries
of service.

July 24, 2022

Lectio Divina for the Seventeenth Week in Ordinary Time

We begin our prayer:

In the name of the Father, and of the Son, and of the Holy Spirit. Amen.

O God, protector of those who hope in you,
without whom nothing has firm foundation, nothing is holy,
bestow in abundance your mercy upon us
and grant that, with you as our ruler and guide,
we may use the good things that pass
in such a way as to hold fast even now
to those that ever endure.
Through our Lord Jesus Christ, your Son,
who lives and reigns with you in the unity of the Holy Spirit,
God, for ever and ever.

Collect, Seventeenth Sunday in Ordinary Time

Reading (*Lectio*)

Read the following Scripture two or three times.

Luke 11:1-13

Jesus was praying in a certain place, and when he had finished, one of his disciples said to him, "Lord, teach us to pray just as John taught his disciples." He said to them, "When you pray, say:

Father, hallowed be your name,
>your kingdom come.
>Give us each day our daily bread
>and forgive us our sins
>for we ourselves forgive everyone in debt to us,
>and do not subject us to the final test."

And he said to them, "Suppose one of you has a friend to whom he goes at midnight and says, 'Friend, lend me three loaves of bread, for a friend of mine has arrived at my house from a journey and I have nothing to offer him,' and he says in reply from within, 'Do not bother me; the door has already been locked and my children and I are already in bed. I cannot get up to give you anything.' I tell you, if he does not get up to give the visitor the loaves because of their friendship, he will get up to give him whatever he needs because of his persistence.

"And I tell you, ask and you will receive; seek and you will find; knock and the door will be opened to you. For everyone who asks, receives; and the one who seeks, finds; and to the one who knocks, the door will be opened. What father among you would hand his son a snake when he asks for a fish? Or hand him a scorpion when he asks for an egg? If you then, who are wicked, know how to give good gifts to your children, how much more will the Father in heaven give the Holy Spirit to those who ask him?"

Meditation (*Meditatio*)

After the reading, take some time to reflect in silence on one or more of the following questions:

- What word or words in this passage caught your attention?
- What in this passage comforted you?
- What in this passage challenged you?

If practicing lectio divina as a family or in a group, after the reflection time, invite the participants to share their responses.

Prayer (*Oratio*)

Read the scripture passage one more time. Bring to the Lord the praise, petition, or thanksgiving that the Word inspires in you.

Contemplation (*Contemplatio*)

Read the Scripture again, followed by this reflection:

≈ What conversion of mind, heart, and life is the Lord asking of me?

_____

_____

_____

_____

≈ *Father, hallowed be your name.* How do I show reverence for the name of God? In what ways do I need to modify my speech to be kinder and more reverent?

_____

_____

_____

_____

≈ *I cannot get up to give you anything.* When have I resisted opportunities to be generous? How can I become more attentive to those in need?

_____

_____

_____

_____

≈ *Ask and you will receive; seek and you will find; knock and the door will be opened to you.* What am I seeking? For what do I need to ask God?

_____

_____

_____

_____

~ *After a period of silent reflection and/or discussion, all recite the Lord's Prayer and the following:*

Closing Prayer

I will give thanks to you, O Lord, with all my heart,
    for you have heard the words of my mouth;
    in the presence of the angels I will sing your praise;
I will worship at your holy temple
    and give thanks to your name.

Because of your kindness and your truth;
    for you have made great above all things
    your name and your promise.
When I called you answered me;
    you built up strength within me.

The Lord is exalted, yet the lowly he sees,
    and the proud he knows from afar.
Though I walk amid distress, you preserve me;
    against the anger of my enemies you raise your hand.

Your right hand saves me.
    The Lord will complete what he has done for me;
your kindness, O Lord, endures forever;
    forsake not the work of your hands.

From Psalm 138

Living the Word This Week

How can I make my life a gift for others in charity?

Read about the Lord's Prayer in the *United States Catholic Catechism for Adults*: *www.usccb.org/sites/default/files/flipbooks/uscca/files/assets/basic-html/page-509.html.*

July 31, 2022

Lectio Divina for the Eighteenth Week in Ordinary Time

We begin our prayer:

In the name of the Father, and of the Son, and of the Holy Spirit. Amen.

Draw near to your servants, O Lord,
and answer their prayers with unceasing kindness,
that, for those who glory in you as their Creator and guide,
you may restore what you have created
and keep safe what you have restored.
Through our Lord Jesus Christ, your Son,
who lives and reigns with you in the unity of the Holy Spirit,
God, for ever and ever

Collect, Eighteenth Sunday in Ordinary Time

Reading (*Lectio*)

Read the following Scripture two or three times.

Luke 12:13-21

> Someone in the crowd said to Jesus, "Teacher, tell my brother to share the inheritance with me." He replied to him, "Friend, who appointed me as your judge and arbitrator?" Then he said to the crowd, "Take care to guard against all greed, for though one may be rich, one's life does not consist of possessions."
>
> Then he told them a parable. "There was a rich man whose land produced a bountiful harvest. He asked himself, 'What shall I do, for I do not have space to store my harvest?' And he said, 'This is what I shall do: I shall tear down my barns and build larger ones. There I shall store all my grain and other goods and I shall say to myself, "Now as for you, you have so many good things stored up for many years, rest, eat, drink, be merry!"' But God said to him, 'You fool, this night your life will be demanded of you; and the things you have prepared, to whom will they belong?' Thus will it be for all who store up treasure for themselves but are not rich in what matters to God."

Meditation (*Meditatio*)

After the reading, take some time to reflect in silence on one or more of the following questions:

- What word or words in this passage caught your attention?
- What in this passage comforted you?
- What in this passage challenged you?

If practicing lectio divina as a family or in a group, after the reflection time, invite the participants to share their responses.

Prayer (*Oratio*)

Read the scripture passage one more time. Bring to the Lord the praise, petition, or thanksgiving that the Word inspires in you.

Contemplation (*Contemplatio*)

Read the Scripture again, followed by this reflection:

≈ What conversion of mind, heart, and life is the Lord asking of me?

_____

_____

_____

_____

≈ *Teacher, tell my brother to share the inheritance with me.* When have I placed burdens on my brothers and sisters? How can I offer correction in a spirit of love and support?

_____

_____

_____

_____

～ *Take care to guard against all greed.* What tempts me to acquire more than I need? How can I grow in detachment from my possessions?

_____

_____

_____

_____

～ *This night your life will be demanded of you.* If today were the final day of my life, how would I live it differently? How am I preparing to meet Jesus at the end of my life?

_____

_____

_____

_____

～ *After a period of silent reflection and/or discussion, all recite the Lord's Prayer and the following:*

Closing Prayer

You turn man back to dust,
    saying, "Return, O children of men."
For a thousand years in your sight
    are as yesterday, now that it is past,
    or as a watch of the night.

You make an end of them in their sleep;
    the next morning they are like the changing grass,
Which at dawn springs up anew,
    but by evening wilts and fades.

Teach us to number our days aright,
    that we may gain wisdom of heart.
Return, O Lord! How long?
    Have pity on your servants!

Fill us at daybreak with your kindness,
    that we may shout for joy and gladness all our days.
And may the gracious care of the Lord our God be ours;
    prosper the work of our hands for us!
    Prosper the work of our hands!

From Psalm 90

Living the Word This Week

How can I make my life a gift for others in charity?

Donate unused possessions or money to an agency that assists the unhoused, refugees, or the formerly incarcerated.

August 7, 2022

Lectio Divina for the Nineteenth Week in Ordinary Time

We begin our prayer:

In the name of the Father, and of the Son, and of the Holy Spirit. Amen.

Almighty ever-living God,
whom, taught by the Holy Spirit,
we dare to call our Father,
bring, we pray, to perfection in our hearts
the spirit of adoption as your sons and daughters,
that we may merit to enter into the inheritance
which you have promised.
Through our Lord Jesus Christ, your Son,
who lives and reigns with you in the unity of the Holy Spirit,
God, for ever and ever.

Collect, Nineteenth Sunday in Ordinary Time

Reading (*Lectio*)

Read the following Scripture two or three times.

Luke 12:32-48 or 12:35-40

Jesus said to his disciples: "Do not be afraid any longer, little flock, for your Father is pleased to give you the kingdom. Sell your belongings and give alms. Provide money bags for yourselves that do not wear out, an inexhaustible treasure in heaven that no thief can reach nor moth destroy. For where your treasure is, there also will your heart be.

"Gird your loins and light your lamps and be like servants who await their master's return from a wedding, ready to open immediately when he comes and knocks. Blessed are those servants whom the master finds vigilant on his arrival. Amen, I say to you, he will gird himself, have them recline at table, and proceed to wait on them. And should he come in the second or third watch and find them prepared in this way, blessed are those servants. Be sure of this: if the master of the house had known the hour when the thief was coming, he would not have let his house be broken into. You also must be prepared, for at an hour you do not expect, the Son of Man will come."

Then Peter said, "Lord, is this parable meant for us or for everyone?" And the Lord replied, "Who, then, is the faithful and prudent steward whom the master will put in charge of his servants to distribute the food allowance at the proper time? Blessed is that servant whom his master on arrival finds doing so. Truly, I say to you, the master will put the servant in charge of all his property. But if that servant says to himself, 'My master is delayed in coming,' and begins to beat the menservants and the maidservants, to eat and drink and get drunk, then that servant's master will come on an unexpected day and at an unknown hour and will punish the servant severely and assign him a place with the unfaithful. That servant who knew his master's will but did not make preparations nor act in accord with his will shall be beaten severely; and the servant who was ignorant of his master's will but acted in a way deserving of a severe beating shall be beaten only lightly. Much will be required of the person entrusted with much, and still more will be demanded of the person entrusted with more."

Meditation (*Meditatio*)

After the reading, take some time to reflect in silence on one or more of the following questions:

- What word or words in this passage caught your attention?
- What in this passage comforted you?
- What in this passage challenged you?

If practicing lectio divina as a family or in a group, after the reflection time, invite the participants to share their responses.

Prayer (*Oratio*)

Read the scripture passage one more time. Bring to the Lord the praise, petition, or thanksgiving that the Word inspires in you.

Contemplation (*Contemplatio*)

Read the Scripture again, followed by this reflection:

~ What conversion of mind, heart, and life is the Lord asking of me?

_____

_____

_____

_____

~ *For where your treasure is, there also will your heart be.* What do I treasure most in life? How do I give evidence to that value?

_____

_____

_____

_____

~ *Gird your loins and light your lamps and be like servants who await their master's return.* How am I preparing for Jesus' return? What steps can I take this week to live a more faith-filled life?

_____

_____

～ *Blessed are those servants whom the master finds vigilant on his arrival.* How do I seek out opportunities to serve? How can I be more diligent in prayer?

_____

_____

_____

_____

～ *After a period of silent reflection and/or discussion, all recite the Lord's Prayer and the following:*

Closing Prayer

Exult, you just, in the LORD;
    praise from the upright is fitting.
Blessed the nation whose God is the LORD,
    the people he has chosen for his own inheritance.

See, the eyes of the LORD are upon those who fear him,
    upon those who hope for his kindness,
To deliver them from death
    and preserve them in spite of famine.

Our soul waits for the LORD,
  who is our help and our shield.
May your kindness, O LORD, be upon us
  who have put our hope in you.

From Psalm 33

Living the Word This Week

How can I make my life a gift for others in charity?

When praying and attending Mass this week, give added effort to being attentive and offering full, conscious, and active participation.

August 14, 2022

Lectio Divina for the Twentieth Week in Ordinary Time

We begin our prayer:

In the name of the Father, and of the Son, and of the Holy Spirit. Amen.

O God, who have prepared for those who love you
good things which no eye can see,
fill our hearts, we pray, with the warmth of your love,
so that, loving you in all things and above all things,
we may attain your promises,
which surpass every human desire.
Through our Lord Jesus Christ, your Son,
who lives and reigns with you in the unity of the Holy Spirit,
God, for ever and ever.

Collect, Twentieth Sunday in Ordinary Time

Reading (*Lectio*)

Read the following Scripture two or three times.

Luke 12:49-53

Jesus said to his disciples: "I have come to set the earth on fire, and how I wish it were already blazing! There is a baptism with which I must be baptized, and how great is my anguish until it is accomplished! Do you think that I have come to establish peace on the earth? No, I tell you, but rather division. From now on a household of five will be divided, three against two and two against three; a father will be divided against his son and a son against his father, a mother against her daughter and a daughter against her mother, a mother-in-law against her daughter-in-law and a daughter-in-law against her mother-in-law."

Meditation (*Meditatio*)

After the reading, take some time to reflect in silence on one or more of the following questions:

- What word or words in this passage caught your attention?
- What in this passage comforted you?
- What in this passage challenged you?

If practicing lectio divina as a family or in a group, after the reflection time, invite the participants to share their responses.

Prayer (*Oratio*)

Read the scripture passage one more time. Bring to the Lord the praise, petition, or thanksgiving that the Word inspires in you.

Contemplation (*Contemplatio*)

Read the Scripture again, followed by this reflection:

≈ What conversion of mind, heart, and life is the Lord asking of me?

_____

_____

_____

_____

≈ *How I wish it were already blazing!* Who in my life is on fire with faith? What inspires me to grow in my spiritual life?

_____

_____

_____

_____

~ *How great is my anguish until it is accomplished!* What in my life is causing emotional pain and suffering? What things have I left undone?

_____

_____

_____

_____

~ *From now on a household of five will be divided.* When has my family or other community suffered from division? With whom do I need to reconcile?

_____

_____

_____

_____

~ *After a period of silent reflection and/or discussion, all recite the Lord's Prayer and the following:*

Closing Prayer

I have waited, waited for the LORD,
    and he stooped toward me.

The LORD heard my cry.
He drew me out of the pit of destruction,
     out of the mud of the swamp;
he set my feet upon a crag;
     he made firm my steps.

And he put a new song into my mouth,
     a hymn to our God.
Many shall look on in awe
     and trust in the LORD.

Though I am afflicted and poor,
     yet the LORD thinks of me.
You are my help and my deliverer;
     O my God, hold not back!

From Psalm 40

Living the Word This Week

How can I make my life a gift for others in charity?

Seek reconciliation with a friend or family member.

August 21, 2022

Lectio Divina for the Twenty-First Week in Ordinary Time

We begin our prayer:

In the name of the Father, and of the Son, and of the Holy Spirit. Amen.

O God, who cause the minds of the faithful
to unite in a single purpose,
grant your people to love what you command
and to desire what you promise,
that, amid the uncertainties of this world,
our hearts may be fixed on that place
where true gladness is found.
Through our Lord Jesus Christ, your Son,
who lives and reigns with you in the unity of the Holy Spirit,
God, for ever and ever.

Collect, Twenty-First Sunday in Ordinary Time

Reading (*Lectio*)

Read the following Scripture two or three times.

Luke 13:22-30

Jesus passed through towns and villages, teaching as he went and making his way to Jerusalem. Someone asked him, "Lord, will only a few people be saved?" He answered them, "Strive to enter through the narrow gate, for many, I tell you, will attempt to enter but will not be strong enough. After the master of the house has arisen and locked the door, then will you stand outside knocking and saying, 'Lord, open the door for us.' He will say to you in reply, 'I do not know where you are from. And you will say, 'We ate and drank in your company and you taught in our streets.' Then he will say to you, 'I do not know where you are from. Depart from me, all you evildoers!' And there will be wailing and grinding of teeth when you see Abraham, Isaac, and Jacob and all the prophets in the kingdom of God and you yourselves cast out. And people will come from the east and the west and from the north and the south and will recline at table in the kingdom of God. For behold, some are last who will be first, and some are first who will be last."

Meditation (*Meditatio*)

After the reading, take some time to reflect in silence on one or more of the following questions:

- What word or words in this passage caught your attention?
- What in this passage comforted you?
- What in this passage challenged you?

If practicing lectio divina as a family or in a group, after the reflection time, invite the participants to share their responses.

Prayer (*Oratio*)

Read the scripture passage one more time. Bring to the Lord the praise, petition, or thanksgiving that the Word inspires in you.

Contemplation (*Contemplatio*)

Read the Scripture again, followed by this reflection:

~ What conversion of mind, heart, and life is the Lord asking of me?

_____

_____

_____

_____

~ *We ate and drank in your company and you taught in our streets.* How can I learn more about my faith? Where do I experience God's presence most profoundly?

_____

_____

_____

_____

∼ *I do not know where you are from.* How do I recognize God's image in those I encounter? How do my actions give testimony to my faith in God?

_____

_____

_____

_____

∼ *And people will come from the east and the west and from the north and the south and will recline at table in the kingdom of God.* How can I be more welcoming to those I meet? What prejudices do I need to remove from my life?

_____

_____

_____

_____

∼ *After a period of silent reflection and/or discussion, all recite the Lord's Prayer and the following:*

Closing Prayer

Praise the LORD all you nations;
glorify him, all you peoples!

For steadfast is his kindness toward us,
  and the fidelity of the LORD endures forever.

From Psalm 117

Living the Word This Week

How can I make my life a gift for others in charity?

Read the U.S. bishops' pastoral statement against racism, *Open Wide Our Hearts: An Enduring Call to Love*: *www.usccb.org/issues-and-action/human-life-and-dignity/racism/upload/open-wide-our-hearts.pdf.*

August 28, 2022

Lectio Divina for the Twenty-Second Week in Ordinary Time

We begin our prayer:

In the name of the Father, and of the Son, and of the Holy Spirit. Amen.

God of might, giver of every good gift,
put into our hearts the love of your name,
so that, by deepening our sense of reverence,
you may nurture in us what is good
and, by your watchful care,
keep safe what you have nurtured.
Through our Lord Jesus Christ, your Son,
who lives and reigns with you in the unity of the Holy Spirit,
God, for ever and ever.

Collect, Twenty-Second Sunday in Ordinary Time

Reading (*Lectio*)

Read the following Scripture two or three times.

Luke 14:1, 7-14

On a sabbath Jesus went to dine at the home of one of the leading Pharisees, and the people there were observing him carefully.

He told a parable to those who had been invited, noticing how they were choosing the places of honor at the table. "When you are invited by someone to a wedding banquet, do not recline at table in the place of honor. A more distinguished guest than you may have been invited by him, and the host who invited both of you may approach you and say, 'Give your place to this man,' and then you would proceed with embarrassment to take the lowest place. Rather, when you are invited, go and take the lowest place so that when the host comes to you he may say, 'My friend, move up to a higher position.' Then you will enjoy the esteem of your companions at the table. For every one who exalts himself will be humbled, but the one who humbles himself will be exalted." Then he said to the host who invited him, "When you hold a lunch or a dinner, do not invite your friends or your brothers or your relatives or your wealthy neighbors, in case they may invite you back and you have repayment. Rather, when you hold a banquet, invite the poor, the crippled, the lame, the blind; blessed indeed will you be because of their inability to repay you. For you will be repaid at the resurrection of the righteous."

Meditation (*Meditatio*)

After the reading, take some time to reflect in silence on one or more of the following questions:

- What word or words in this passage caught your attention?
- What in this passage comforted you?
- What in this passage challenged you?

If practicing lectio divina as a family or in a group, after the reflection time, invite the participants to share their responses.

Prayer (*Oratio*)

Read the scripture passage one more time. Bring to the Lord the praise, petition, or thanksgiving that the Word inspires in you.

Contemplation (*Contemplatio*)

Read the Scripture again, followed by this reflection:

~ What conversion of mind, heart, and life is the Lord asking of me?

_____

_____

_____

_____

≈ *He told a parable to those who had been invited, noticing how they were choosing the places of honor at the table.* When have I sought worldly acclaim and honor? Who have I excluded?

_____

_____

_____

_____

≈ *Give your place to this man.* For whom am I willing to make sacrifices? How can I expand that circle?

_____

_____

_____

_____

≈ *For every one who exalts himself will be humbled, but the one who humbles himself will be exalted.* When have I committed the sin of pride? How can I grow in humility?

_____

_____

_____

_____

~ After a period of silent reflection and/or discussion, all recite the Lord's Prayer and the following:

Closing Prayer

The just rejoice and exult before God;
    they are glad and rejoice.
Sing to God, chant praise to his name,
    whose name is the LORD.

The father of orphans and the defender of widows
    is God in his holy dwelling.
God gives a home to the forsaken;
    he leads forth prisoners to prosperity.

A bountiful rain you showered down, O God, upon your inheritance;
    you restored the land when it languished;
your flock settled in it;
    in your goodness, O God, you provided it for the needy.

From Psalm 68

Living the Word This Week

How can I make my life a gift for others in charity?

Make an examination of conscience in light of Catholic social teaching (*www.usccb.org/prayer-and-worship/sacraments-and-sacramentals/ penance/examination-conscience-in-light-of-catholic-social-teaching*) and receive the Sacrament of Penance.

September 4, 2022

Lectio Divina for the Twenty-Third Week in Ordinary Time

We begin our prayer:

In the name of the Father, and of the Son, and of the Holy Spirit. Amen.

O God, by whom we are redeemed and receive adoption,
look graciously upon your beloved sons and daughters,
that those who believe in Christ
may receive true freedom
and an everlasting inheritance.
Through our Lord Jesus Christ, your Son,
who lives and reigns with you in the unity of the Holy Spirit,
God, for ever and ever.

Collect, Twenty-Third Sunday in Ordinary Time

Reading (*Lectio*)

Read the following Scripture two or three times.

Luke 14:25-33

Great crowds were traveling with Jesus, and he turned and addressed them, "If anyone comes to me without hating his father and mother, wife and children, brothers and sisters, and even his own life, he cannot be my disciple. Whoever does not carry his own cross and come after me cannot be my disciple. Which of you wishing to construct a tower does not first sit down and calculate the cost to see if there is enough for its completion? Otherwise, after laying the foundation and finding himself unable to finish the work the onlookers should laugh at him and say, 'This one began to build but did not have the resources to finish.' Or what king marching into battle would not first sit down and decide whether with ten thousand troops he can successfully oppose another king advancing upon him with twenty thousand troops? But if not, while he is still far away, he will send a delegation to ask for peace terms. In the same way, anyone of you who does not renounce all his possessions cannot be my disciple."

Meditation (*Meditatio*)

After the reading, take some time to reflect in silence on one or more of the following questions:

- What word or words in this passage caught your attention?
- What in this passage comforted you?
- What in this passage challenged you?

If practicing lectio divina as a family or in a group, after the reflection time, invite the participants to share their responses.

Prayer (*Oratio*)

Read the scripture passage one more time. Bring to the Lord the praise, petition, or thanksgiving that the Word inspires in you.

Contemplation (*Contemplatio*)

Read the Scripture again, followed by this reflection:

~ What conversion of mind, heart, and life is the Lord asking of me?

~ *If anyone comes to me without hating . . . even his own life, he cannot be my disciple.* How do I show that God is my utmost priority? What am I willing to give up for my faith?

≈ *This one began to build but did not have the resources to finish.* Who helped to establish my foundation in faith? What resources do I need to build on that foundation?

_____

_____

_____

_____

≈ *While he is still far away, he will send a delegation to ask for peace terms.* What are the sources of division in my family and community? How can I be a peacemaker in my family and community?

_____

_____

_____

_____

≈ *After a period of silent reflection and/or discussion, all recite the Lord's Prayer and the following:*

Closing Prayer

You turn man back to dust,
    saying, "Return, O children of men."
For a thousand years in your sight
    are as yesterday, now that it is past,
    or as a watch of the night.

You make an end of them in their sleep;
    the next morning they are like the changing grass,
Which at dawn springs up anew,
    but by evening wilts and fades.

Teach us to number our days aright,
    that we may gain wisdom of heart.
Return, O Lord! How long?
    Have pity on your servants!

Fill us at daybreak with your kindness,
    that we may shout for joy and gladness all our days.
And may the gracious care of the Lord our God be ours;
    prosper the work of our hands for us!
    Prosper the work of our hands!

From Psalm 90

Living the Word This Week

How can I make my life a gift for others in charity?

Fast from food or another pleasure for a day and offer it up for the peace of the world.

September 11, 2022

Lectio Divina for the Twenty-Fourth Week in Ordinary Time

We begin our prayer:

In the name of the Father, and of the Son, and of the Holy Spirit. Amen.

Look upon us, O God,
Creator and ruler of all things,
and, that we may feel the working of your mercy,
grant that we may serve you with all our heart.
Through our Lord Jesus Christ, your Son,
who lives and reigns with you in the unity of the Holy Spirit,
God, for ever and ever.

Collect, Twenty-Fourth Sunday in Ordinary Time

Reading (*Lectio*)

Read the following Scripture two or three times.

Luke 15:1-10 or 15:1-32

Tax collectors and sinners were all drawing near to listen to Jesus, but the Pharisees and scribes began to complain, saying, "This man welcomes sinners and eats with them." So to them he addressed this parable. "What man among you having a hundred sheep and losing one of them would not leave the ninety-nine in the desert and go after the lost one until he finds it? And when he does find it, he sets it on his shoulders with great joy and, upon his arrival home, he calls together his friends and neighbors and says to them, 'Rejoice with me because I have found my lost sheep.' I tell you, in just the same way there will be more joy in heaven over one sinner who repents than over ninety-nine righteous people who have no need of repentance.

"Or what woman having ten coins and losing one would not light a lamp and sweep the house, searching carefully until she finds it? And when she does find it, she calls together her friends and neighbors and says to them, 'Rejoice with me because I have found the coin that I lost.' In just the same way, I tell you, there will be rejoicing among the angels of God over one sinner who repents."

Meditation (*Meditatio*)

After the reading, take some time to reflect in silence on one or more of the following questions:

- What word or words in this passage caught your attention?
- What in this passage comforted you?
- What in this passage challenged you?

If practicing lectio divina as a family or in a group, after the reflection time, invite the participants to share their responses.

Prayer (*Oratio*)

Read the scripture passage one more time. Bring to the Lord the praise, petition, or thanksgiving that the Word inspires in you.

Contemplation (*Contemplatio*)

Read the Scripture again, followed by this reflection:

≈ What conversion of mind, heart, and life is the Lord asking of me?

~ *Tax collectors and sinners were all drawing near to listen to Jesus, but the Pharisees and scribes began to complain.* Where can I draw near to listen to Jesus? When has my behavior or attitude kept others from hearing Jesus?

_____

_____

_____

_____

~ *He calls together his friends and neighbors and says to them, "Rejoice with me because I have found my lost sheep."* When have I shared my faith with my friends and neighbors? How does my life testify to the joy of the Gospel?

_____

_____

_____

_____

~ *Or what woman having ten coins and losing one would not light a lamp and sweep the house, searching carefully until she finds it?* For what am I searching? How can the Church and her teaching give light to my search?

_____

_____

_____

_____

∼ *After a period of silent reflection and/or discussion, all recite the Lord's Prayer and the following:*

Closing Prayer

Have mercy on me, O God, in your goodness;
   in the greatness of your compassion wipe out my offense.
Thoroughly wash me from my guilt
   and of my sin cleanse me.

A clean heart create for me, O God,
   and a steadfast spirit renew within me.
Cast me not out from your presence,
   and your Holy Spirit take not from me.

O Lord, open my lips,
   and my mouth shall proclaim your praise.
My sacrifice, O God, is a contrite spirit;
   a heart contrite and humbled, O God, you will not spurn.

From Psalm 51

Living the Word This Week

How can I make my life a gift for others in charity?

Read chapter 5 of *The Joy of the Gospel* (*Evangelii Gaudium*): *www.vatican.va/content/francesco/en/apost_exhortations/documents/papa-francesco_esortazione-ap_20131124_evangelii-gaudium.html.*

September 18, 2022

Lectio Divina for the Twenty-Fifth Week in Ordinary Time

We begin our prayer:

In the name of the Father, and of the Son, and of the Holy Spirit. Amen.

O God, who founded all the commands of your sacred Law
upon love of you and of our neighbor,
grant that, by keeping your precepts,
we may merit to attain eternal life.
Through our Lord Jesus Christ, your Son,
who lives and reigns with you in the unity of the Holy Spirit,
God, for ever and ever.

Collect, Twenty-Fifth Sunday in Ordinary Time

Reading (*Lectio*)

Read the following Scripture two or three times.

Luke 16:1-13 or 16:10-13

Jesus said to his disciples, "A rich man had a steward who was reported to him for squandering his property. He summoned him and said, 'What is this I hear about you? Prepare a full account of your stewardship, because you can no longer be my steward.' The steward said to himself, 'What shall I do, now that my master is taking the position of steward away from me? I am not strong enough to dig and I am ashamed to beg. I know what I shall do so that, when I am removed from the stewardship, they may welcome me into their homes.' He called in his master's debtors one by one. To the first he said, 'How much do you owe my master?' He replied, 'One hundred measures of olive oil.' He said to him, 'Here is your promissory note. Sit down and quickly write one for fifty.' Then to another the steward said, 'And you, how much do you owe?' He replied, 'One hundred kors of wheat.' The steward said to him, 'Here is your promissory note; write one for eighty.' And the master commended that dishonest steward for acting prudently. "For the children of this world are more prudent in dealing with their own generation than are the children of light. I tell you, make friends for yourselves with dishonest wealth, so that when it fails, you will be welcomed into eternal dwellings. The person who is trustworthy in very small matters is also trustworthy in great ones; and the person who is dishonest in very small matters is also dishonest in great ones. If, therefore, you are not trustworthy with dishonest wealth, who will trust you with true wealth? If you are not trustworthy with what belongs to another, who will give you what is yours? No servant can serve two masters. He will either hate one and love the other, or be devoted to one and despise the other. You cannot serve both God and mammon."

Meditation (*Meditatio*)

After the reading, take some time to reflect in silence on one or more of the following questions:

- What word or words in this passage caught your attention?
- What in this passage comforted you?
- What in this passage challenged you?

If practicing lectio divina as a family or in a group, after the reflection time, invite the participants to share their responses.

Prayer (*Oratio*)

Read the scripture passage one more time. Bring to the Lord the praise, petition, or thanksgiving that the Word inspires in you.

Contemplation (*Contemplatio*)

Read the Scripture again, followed by this reflection:

∿ What conversion of mind, heart, and life is the Lord asking of me?

_____

_____

_____

_____

≈ *I know what I shall do so that, when I am removed from the stewardship, they may welcome me into their homes.* How do I accept hospitality? How do I show others hospitality, especially those on the peripheries?

_____

_____

_____

_____

≈ *If, therefore, you are not trustworthy with dishonest wealth, who will trust you with true wealth?* What is my true wealth? How do I steward this wealth with care?

_____

_____

_____

_____

≈ *No servant can serve two masters.* Whom do I serve? How is that service shown in my daily life?

_____

_____

_____

_____

≈ After a period of silent reflection and/or discussion, all recite the Lord's Prayer and the following:

Closing Prayer

Praise, you servants of the LORD,
    praise the name of the LORD.
Blessed be the name of the LORD
    both now and forever.

High above all nations is the LORD;
    above the heavens is his glory.
Who is like the LORD, our God, who is enthroned on high
    and looks upon the heavens and the earth below?

He raises up the lowly from the dust;
    from the dunghill he lifts up the poor
to seat them with princes,
    with the princes of his own people.

From Psalm 113

Living the Word This Week

How can I make my life a gift for others in charity?

Learn about social justice initiatives in your parish and diocese and consider prayerfully how you might participate.

September 25, 2022

Lectio Divina for the Twenty-Sixth Week in Ordinary Time

We begin our prayer:

In the name of the Father, and of the Son, and of the Holy Spirit. Amen.

O God, who manifest your almighty power
above all by pardoning and showing mercy,
bestow, we pray, your grace abundantly upon us
and make those hastening to attain your promises
heirs to the treasures of heaven.
Through our Lord Jesus Christ, your Son,
who lives and reigns with you in the unity of the Holy Spirit,
God, for ever and ever.

Collect, Twenty-Sixth Sunday in Ordinary Time

Reading (*Lectio*)

Read the following Scripture two or three times.

Luke 16:19-31

Jesus said to the Pharisees: "There was a rich man who dressed in purple garments and fine linen and dined sumptuously each day. And lying at his door was a poor man named Lazarus, covered with sores, who would gladly have eaten his fill of the scraps that fell from the rich man's table. Dogs even used to come and lick his sores. When the poor man died, he was carried away by angels to the bosom of Abraham. The rich man also died and was buried, and from the netherworld, where he was in torment, he raised his eyes and saw Abraham far off and Lazarus at his side. And he cried out, 'Father Abraham, have pity on me. Send Lazarus to dip the tip of his finger in water and cool my tongue, for I am suffering torment in these flames.' Abraham replied, 'My child, remember that you received what was good during your lifetime while Lazarus likewise received what was bad; but now he is comforted here, whereas you are tormented. Moreover, between us and you a great chasm is established to prevent anyone from crossing who might wish to go from our side to yours or from your side to ours.' He said, 'Then I beg you, father, send him to my father's house, for I have five brothers, so that he may warn them, lest they too come to this place of torment.' But Abraham replied, 'They have Moses and the prophets. Let them listen to them.' He said, 'Oh no, father Abraham, but if someone from the dead goes to them, they will repent.' Then Abraham said, 'If they will not listen to Moses and the prophets, neither will they be persuaded if someone should rise from the dead.'"

Meditation (*Meditatio*)

After the reading, take some time to reflect in silence on one or more of the following questions:

- What word or words in this passage caught your attention?
- What in this passage comforted you?
- What in this passage challenged you?

If practicing lectio divina as a family or in a group, after the reflection time, invite the participants to share their responses.

Prayer (*Oratio*)

Read the scripture passage one more time. Bring to the Lord the praise, petition, or thanksgiving that the Word inspires in you.

Contemplation (*Contemplatio*)

Read the Scripture again, followed by this reflection:

≈ What conversion of mind, heart, and life is the Lord asking of me?

_____

_____

_____

_____

~ *Father Abraham, have pity on me. Send Lazarus to dip the tip of his finger in water and cool my tongue, for I am suffering torment in these flames.* For what do I need to ask God for his pity and compassion? How can I bring comfort to those who are suffering?

_____

_____

_____

_____

~ *My child, remember that you received what was good during your lifetime.* What good things has God given me in my lifetime? How can I be more generous in sharing these gifts?

_____

_____

_____

_____

~ *If they will not listen to Moses and the prophets, neither will they be persuaded if someone should rise from the dead.* What preaching do I find most persuasive? To whom do I listen?

_____

_____

~ *After a period of silent reflection and/or discussion, all recite the Lord's Prayer and the following:*

Closing Prayer

Blessed he who keeps faith forever,
>   secures justice for the oppressed,
>   gives food to the hungry.
The Lord sets captives free.

The Lord gives sight to the blind.
>   The Lord raises up those who were bowed down;
the Lord loves the just.
>   The Lord protects strangers.

The fatherless and the widow he sustains,
>   but the way of the wicked he thwarts.
The Lord shall reign forever;
>   your God, O Zion, through all generations. Alleluia.

From Psalm 146

Living the Word This Week

How can I make my life a gift for others in charity?

Perform one (or more) of the corporal works of mercy.

October 2, 2022

Lectio Divina for the Twenty-Seventh Week in Ordinary Time

We begin our prayer:

In the name of the Father, and of the Son, and of the Holy Spirit. Amen.

Almighty ever-living God,
who in the abundance of your kindness
surpass the merits and the desires of those who entreat you,
pour out your mercy upon us
to pardon what conscience dreads
and to give what prayer does not dare to ask.
Through our Lord Jesus Christ, your Son,
who lives and reigns with you in the unity of the Holy Spirit,
God, for ever and ever.

Collect, Twenty-Seventh Sunday in Ordinary Time

Reading (*Lectio*)

Read the following Scripture two or three times.

Luke 17:5-10

> The apostles said to the Lord, "Increase our faith." The Lord replied, "If you have faith the size of a mustard seed, you would say to this mulberry tree, 'Be uprooted and planted in the sea,' and it would obey you.

> "Who among you would say to your servant who has just come in from plowing or tending sheep in the field, 'Come here immediately and take your place at table'? Would he not rather say to him, 'Prepare something for me to eat. Put on your apron and wait on me while I eat and drink. You may eat and drink when I am finished'? Is he grateful to that servant because he did what was commanded? So should it be with you. When you have done all you have been commanded, say, 'We are unprofitable servants; we have done what we were obliged to do.'"

Meditation (*Meditatio*)

After the reading, take some time to reflect in silence on one or more of the following questions:

- What word or words in this passage caught your attention?
- What in this passage comforted you?
- What in this passage challenged you?

If practicing lectio divina as a family or in a group, after the reflection time, invite the participants to share their responses.

Prayer (*Oratio*)

Read the scripture passage one more time. Bring to the Lord the praise, petition, or thanksgiving that the Word inspires in you.

Contemplation (*Contemplatio*)

Read the Scripture again, followed by this reflection:

~ What conversion of mind, heart, and life is the Lord asking of me?

_____

_____

_____

_____

~ *If you have faith the size of a mustard seed. . . .* How am I nurturing the seed of my faith? What resources do I have that can strengthen my faith?

_____

_____

_____

_____

≈ *Come here immediately and take your place at table.* To what is God calling me? Who needs to be invited to the table?

_____

_____

_____

_____

≈ *When you have done all you have been commanded. . . .* How faithfully do I live the commandments? What sinful behavior do I need to bring to God for healing?

_____

_____

_____

_____

≈ *After a period of silent reflection and/or discussion, all recite the Lord's Prayer and the following:*

Closing Prayer

Come, let us sing joyfully to the LORD;
    let us acclaim the Rock of our salvation.
Let us come into his presence with thanksgiving;
    let us joyfully sing psalms to him.

Come, let us bow down in worship;
 let us kneel before the LORD who made us.
For he is our God,
 and we are the people he shepherds, the flock he guides.

Oh, that today you would hear his voice:
 "Harden not your hearts as at Meribah,
 as in the day of Massah in the desert,
Where your fathers tempted me;
 they tested me though they had seen my works."

From Psalm 95

Living the Word This Week

How can I make my life a gift for others in charity?

Before bed each night, review your day to discern how faithfully you followed the commandments and lived your faith and to recognize when God was present.

October 9, 2022

Lectio Divina for the Twenty-Eighth Week in Ordinary Time

We begin our prayer:

In the name of the Father, and of the Son, and of the Holy Spirit. Amen.

May your grace, O Lord, we pray,
at all times go before us and follow after
and make us always determined
to carry out good works.
Through our Lord Jesus Christ, your Son,
who lives and reigns with you in the unity of the Holy Spirit,
God, for ever and ever.

Collect, Twenty-Eighth Sunday in Ordinary Time

Reading (*Lectio*)

Read the following Scripture two or three times.

Luke 17:11-19

> As Jesus continued his journey to Jerusalem, he traveled through Samaria and Galilee. As he was entering a village, ten lepers met him. They stood at a distance from him and raised their voices, saying, "Jesus, Master! Have pity on us!" And when he saw them, he said, "Go show yourselves to the priests." As they were going they were cleansed. And one of them, realizing he had been healed, returned, glorifying God in a loud voice; and he fell at the feet of Jesus and thanked him. He was a Samaritan. Jesus said in reply, "Ten were cleansed, were they not? Where are the other nine? Has none but this foreigner returned to give thanks to God?" Then he said to him, "Stand up and go; your faith has saved you."

Meditation (*Meditatio*)

After the reading, take some time to reflect in silence on one or more of the following questions:

- What word or words in this passage caught your attention?
- What in this passage comforted you?
- What in this passage challenged you?

If practicing lectio divina as a family or in a group, after the reflection time, invite the participants to share their responses.

Prayer (*Oratio*)

Read the scripture passage one more time. Bring to the Lord the praise, petition, or thanksgiving that the Word inspires in you.

Contemplation (*Contemplatio*)

Read the Scripture again, followed by this reflection:

～ What conversion of mind, heart, and life is the Lord asking of me?

_____

_____

_____

_____

～ *As Jesus continued his journey to Jerusalem, he traveled through Samaria and Galilee.* Where am I on my spiritual journey? What pitfalls do I face on this journey?

_____

_____

_____

_____

~ *As they were going they were cleansed.* From what do I need to be cleansed? What near occasions of sin must I avoid?

_____

_____

_____

_____

~ *He fell at the feet of Jesus and thanked him.* How do I express my gratitude to God? How do I show God reverence and adoration?

_____

_____

_____

_____

~ *After a period of silent reflection and/or discussion, all recite the Lord's Prayer and the following:*

Closing Prayer

Sing to the LORD a new song,
   for he has done wondrous deeds;
his right hand has won victory for him,
   his holy arm.

The Lord has made his salvation known:
  in the sight of the nations he has revealed his justice.
He has remembered his kindness and his faithfulness
  toward the house of Israel.

All the ends of the earth have seen
  the salvation by our God.
Sing joyfully to the Lord, all you lands:
  break into song; sing praise.

From Psalm 98

Living the Word This Week

How can I make my life a gift for others in charity?

Set up a crucifix in your home and pray before it each day for a spirit
of conversion and gratitude.

October 16, 2022

Lectio Divina for the Twenty-Ninth Week in Ordinary Time

We begin our prayer:

In the name of the Father, and of the Son, and of the Holy Spirit. Amen.

Almighty ever-living God,
grant that we may always conform our will to yours
and serve your majesty in sincerity of heart.
Through our Lord Jesus Christ, your Son,
who lives and reigns with you in the unity of the Holy Spirit,
God, for ever and ever.

Collect, Twenty-Ninth Sunday in Ordinary Time

Reading (*Lectio*)

Read the following Scripture two or three times.

Luke 18:1-8

> Jesus told his disciples a parable about the necessity for them to pray always without becoming weary. He said, "There was a judge in a certain town who neither feared God nor respected any human being. And a widow in that town used to come to him and say, 'Render a just decision for me against my adversary.' For a long time the judge was unwilling, but eventually he thought, 'While it is true that I neither fear God nor respect any human being, because this widow keeps bothering me I shall deliver a just decision for her lest she finally come and strike me.'" The Lord said, "Pay attention to what the dishonest judge says. Will not God then secure the rights of his chosen ones who call out to him day and night? Will he be slow to answer them? I tell you, he will see to it that justice is done for them speedily. But when the Son of Man comes, will he find faith on earth?"

Meditation (*Meditatio*)

After the reading, take some time to reflect in silence on one or more of the following questions:

- What word or words in this passage caught your attention?
- What in this passage comforted you?
- What in this passage challenged you?

If practicing lectio divina as a family or in a group, after the reflection time, invite the participants to share their responses.

Prayer (*Oratio*)

Read the scripture passage one more time. Bring to the Lord the praise, petition, or thanksgiving that the Word inspires in you.

Contemplation (*Contemplatio*)

Read the Scripture again, followed by this reflection:

≈ What conversion of mind, heart, and life is the Lord asking of me?

_____

_____

_____

_____

≈ *There was a judge in a certain town who neither feared God nor respected any human being.* How do I understand the Holy Spirit's gift of fear of the Lord? How can I be more intentional about seeing God's image in each person that I meet?

_____

_____

_____

_____

≈ *Render a just decision for me against my adversary.* When have I suffered an injustice? How did I respond to that injustice in light of my faith?

_____

_____

_____

_____

≈ *Will* [God] *be slow to answer them?* For what do I need to ask God today? How do I respond when God does not respond to my prayers on my timetable?

_____

_____

_____

_____

≈ *After a period of silent reflection and/or discussion, all recite the Lord's Prayer and the following:*

Closing Prayer

I lift up my eyes toward the mountains;
   whence shall help come to me?
My help is from the LORD,
   who made heaven and earth.

May he not suffer your foot to slip;
   may he slumber not who guards you:
indeed he neither slumbers nor sleeps,
   the guardian of Israel.

The LORD is your guardian; the LORD is your shade;
   he is beside you at your right hand.
The sun shall not harm you by day,
   nor the moon by night.

The LORD will guard you from all evil;
   he will guard your life.
The LORD will guard your coming and your going,
   both now and forever.

From Psalm 121

Living the Word This Week

How can I make my life a gift for others in charity?

Pray for just and compassionate decision-making from all those involved in the administration of justice.

October 23, 2022

Lectio Divina for the Thirtieth Week in Ordinary Time

We begin our prayer:

In the name of the Father, and of the Son, and of the Holy Spirit. Amen.

Almighty ever-living God,
increase our faith, hope and charity,
and make us love what you command,
so that we may merit what you promise.
Through our Lord Jesus Christ, your Son,
who lives and reigns with you in the unity of the Holy Spirit,
God, for ever and ever.

Collect, Thirtieth Sunday in Ordinary Time

Reading (*Lectio*)

Read the following Scripture two or three times.

Luke 18:9-14

Jesus addressed this parable to those who were convinced of their own righteousness and despised everyone else. "Two people went up to the temple area to pray; one was a Pharisee and the other was a tax collector. The Pharisee took up his position and spoke this prayer to himself, 'O God, I thank you that I am not like the rest of humanity—greedy, dishonest, adulterous—or even like this tax collector. I fast twice a week, and I pay tithes on my whole income.' But the tax collector stood off at a distance and would not even raise his eyes to heaven but beat his breast and prayed, 'O God, be merciful to me a sinner.' I tell you, the latter went home justified, not the former; for whoever exalts himself will be humbled, and the one who humbles himself will be exalted."

Meditation (*Meditatio*)

After the reading, take some time to reflect in silence on one or more of the following questions:

- What word or words in this passage caught your attention?
- What in this passage comforted you?
- What in this passage challenged you?

If practicing lectio divina as a family or in a group, after the reflection time, invite the participants to share their responses.

Prayer (*Oratio*)

Read the scripture passage one more time. Bring to the Lord the praise, petition, or thanksgiving that the Word inspires in you.

Contemplation (*Contemplatio*)

Read the Scripture again, followed by this reflection:

≈ What conversion of mind, heart, and life is the Lord asking of me?

_____

_____

_____

_____

≈ *Two people went up to the temple area to pray.* Where do I go to pray? What can I do to strengthen my prayer life?

_____

_____

_____

_____

≈ *O God, I thank you that I am not like the rest of humanity.* What people or groups do I judge? Whom do I exclude from my circle of love?

_____

_____

_____

_____

≈ *O God, be merciful to me a sinner.* For what sins must I repent? How can I open my heart to God's gift of mercy?

_____

_____

_____

_____

≈ *After a period of silent reflection and/or discussion, all recite the Lord's Prayer and the following:*

Closing Prayer

I will bless the LORD at all times;
    his praise shall be ever in my mouth.
Let my soul glory in the LORD;
    the lowly will hear me and be glad.

The LORD confronts the evildoers,
>   to destroy remembrance of them from the earth.
When the just cry out, the Lord hears them,
>   and from all their distress he rescues them.

The LORD is close to the brokenhearted;
>   and those who are crushed in spirit he saves.
The LORD redeems the lives of his servants;
>   no one incurs guilt who takes refuge in him.

From Psalm 34

Living the Word This Week

How can I make my life a gift for others in charity?

Celebrate God's merciful love by receiving the Sacrament of Penance.

October 30, 2022

Lectio Divina for the Thirty-First Week in Ordinary Time

We begin our prayer:

In the name of the Father, and of the Son, and of the Holy Spirit. Amen.

Almighty and merciful God,
by whose gift your faithful offer you
right and praiseworthy service,
grant, we pray,
that we may hasten without stumbling
to receive the things you have promised.
Through our Lord Jesus Christ, your Son,
who lives and reigns with you in the unity of the Holy Spirit,
God, for ever and ever.

Collect, Thirty-First Sunday in Ordinary Time

Reading (*Lectio*)

Read the following Scripture two or three times.

Luke 19:1-10

> At that time, Jesus came to Jericho and intended to pass through the town. Now a man there named Zacchaeus, who was a chief tax collector and also a wealthy man, was seeking to see who Jesus was; but he could not see him because of the crowd, for he was short in stature. So he ran ahead and climbed a sycamore tree in order to see Jesus, who was about to pass that way. When he reached the place, Jesus looked up and said, "Zacchaeus, come down quickly, for today I must stay at your house." And he came down quickly and received him with joy. When they all saw this, they began to grumble, saying, "He has gone to stay at the house of a sinner." But Zacchaeus stood there and said to the Lord, "Behold, half of my possessions, Lord, I shall give to the poor, and if I have extorted anything from anyone I shall repay it four times over." And Jesus said to him, "Today salvation has come to this house because this man too is a descendant of Abraham. For the Son of Man has come to seek and to save what was lost."

Meditation (*Meditatio*)

After the reading, take some time to reflect in silence on one or more of the following questions:

- What word or words in this passage caught your attention?
- What in this passage comforted you?
- What in this passage challenged you?

If practicing lectio divina as a family or in a group, after the reflection time, invite the participants to share their responses.

Prayer (*Oratio*)

Read the scripture passage one more time. Bring to the Lord the praise, petition, or thanksgiving that the Word inspires in you.

Contemplation (*Contemplatio*)

Read the Scripture again, followed by this reflection:

∿ What conversion of mind, heart, and life is the Lord asking of me?

\
\
\
\

∿ *So he ran ahead and climbed a sycamore tree in order to see Jesus, who was about to pass that way.* What can I do to seek the Lord more intently? How can I grow in discipleship?

\
\
\
\

~ *Behold, half of my possessions, Lord, I shall give to the poor.* How can I respond to the immediate needs of those who are poor? How can I address the structures of sin that keep people in poverty?

_____

_____

_____

_____

~ *Today salvation has come to this house.* How have I experienced God's presence and action today? How can I help others come to know God's saving action?

_____

_____

_____

_____

~ *After a period of silent reflection and/or discussion, all recite the Lord's Prayer and the following:*

Closing Prayer

I will extol you, O my God and King,
    and I will bless your name forever and ever.
Every day will I bless you,
    and I will praise your name forever and ever.

The Lord is gracious and merciful,
  slow to anger and of great kindness.
The Lord is good to all
  and compassionate toward all his works.

Let all your works give you thanks, O Lord,
  and let your faithful ones bless you.
Let them discourse of the glory of your kingdom
  and speak of your might.

The Lord is faithful in all his words
  and holy in all his works.
The Lord lifts up all who are falling
  and raises up all who are bowed down.

From Psalm 145

Living the Word This Week

How can I make my life a gift for others in charity?

Learn more about putting the two feet of love in action: *www.usccb. org/beliefs-and-teachings/what-we-believe/catholic-social-teaching/ two-feet-of-love-in-action.*

November 1, 2022

Lectio Divina for the Solemnity of All Saints

We begin our prayer:

In the name of the Father, and of the Son, and of the Holy Spirit. Amen.

Almighty ever-living God,
by whose gift we venerate in one celebration
the merits of all the Saints,
bestow on us, we pray,
through the prayers of so many intercessors,
an abundance of the reconciliation with you
for which we earnestly long.
Through our Lord Jesus Christ, your Son,
who lives and reigns with you in the unity of the Holy Spirit,
God, for ever and ever.

Collect, Solemnity of All Saints

Reading (*Lectio*)

Read the following Scripture two or three times.

Matthew 5:1-12a

When Jesus saw the crowds, he went up the mountain, and after he had sat down, his disciples came to him. He began to teach them, saying:

"Blessed are the poor in spirit,
   for theirs is the Kingdom of heaven.
Blessed are they who mourn,
   for they will be comforted.
Blessed are the meek,
   for they will inherit the land.
Blessed are they who hunger and thirst for righteousness,
   for they will be satisfied.
Blessed are the merciful,
   for they will be shown mercy.
Blessed are the clean of heart,
   for they will see God.
Blessed are the peacemakers,
   for they will be called children of God.
Blessed are they who are persecuted for the sake of righteousness,
   for theirs is the Kingdom of heaven.
Blessed are you when they insult you and persecute you
   and utter every kind of evil against you falsely because of me.
Rejoice and be glad,
   for your reward will be great in heaven."

Meditation (*Meditatio*)

After the reading, take some time to reflect in silence on one or more of the following questions:

- What word or words in this passage caught your attention?
- What in this passage comforted you?
- What in this passage challenged you?

If practicing lectio divina as a family or in a group, after the reflection time, invite the participants to share their responses.

Prayer (*Oratio*)

Read the scripture passage one more time. Bring to the Lord the praise, petition, or thanksgiving that the Word inspires in you.

Contemplation (*Contemplatio*)

Read the Scripture again, followed by this reflection:

≈ What conversion of mind, heart, and life is the Lord asking of me?

∼ *Blessed are they who mourn, / for they will be comforted.* Whom do I know who is mourning? What practical offers of comfort can I make to assist them?

_____

_____

_____

_____

∼ *Blessed are the meek, / for they will inherit the land.* How can I grow in humility? How can I show greater respect for and care of the earth and its resources?

_____

_____

_____

_____

∼ *Blessed are the peacemakers, / for they will be called children of God.* What things disturb the peace of my family, my community, the world? How can I be a force for peace?

_____

_____

_____

_____

~ *After a period of silent reflection and/or discussion, all recite the Lord's Prayer and the following:*

Closing Prayer

The LORD's are the earth and its fullness;
    the world and those who dwell in it.
For he founded it upon the seas
    and established it upon the rivers.

Who can ascend the mountain of the LORD?
    or who may stand in his holy place?
One whose hands are sinless, whose heart is clean,
    who desires not what is vain.

He shall receive a blessing from the LORD,
    a reward from God his savior.
Such is the race that seeks him,
    that seeks the face of the God of Jacob.

From Psalm 24

Living the Word This Week

How can I make my life a gift for others in charity?

Pray with the news each day this week, offering your prayers and sacrifices for the needs in each day's top news stories.

November 6, 2022

Lectio Divina for the Thirty-Second Week in Ordinary Time

We begin our prayer:

In the name of the Father, and of the Son, and of the Holy Spirit. Amen.

Almighty and merciful God,
graciously keep from us all adversity,
so that, unhindered in mind and body alike,
we may pursue in freedom of heart
the things that are yours.
Through our Lord Jesus Christ, your Son,
who lives and reigns with you in the unity of the Holy Spirit,
God, for ever and ever.

Collect, Thirty-Second Sunday in Ordinary Time

Reading (*Lectio*)

Read the following Scripture two or three times.

Luke 20:27-38

Some Sadducees, those who deny that there is a resurrection, came forward and put this question to Jesus, saying, "Teacher, Moses wrote for us, *If someone's brother dies leaving a wife but no child, his brother must take the wife and raise up descendants for his brother.* Now there were seven brothers; the first married a woman but died childless. Then the second and the third married her, and likewise all the seven died childless. Finally the woman also died. Now at the resurrection whose wife will that woman be? For all seven had been married to her." Jesus said to them, "The children of this age marry and remarry; but those who are deemed worthy to attain to the coming age and to the resurrection of the dead neither marry nor are given in marriage. They can no longer die, for they are like angels; and they are the children of God because they are the ones who will rise. That the dead will rise even Moses made known in the passage about the bush, when he called out 'Lord,' the God of Abraham, the God of Isaac, and the God of Jacob; and he is not God of the dead, but of the living, for to him all are alive."

Meditation (*Meditatio*)

After the reading, take some time to reflect in silence on one or more of the following questions:

- What word or words in this passage caught your attention?
- What in this passage comforted you?
- What in this passage challenged you?

If practicing lectio divina as a family or in a group, after the reflection time, invite the participants to share their responses.

Prayer (*Oratio*)

Read the scripture passage one more time. Bring to the Lord the praise, petition, or thanksgiving that the Word inspires in you.

Contemplation (*Contemplatio*)

Read the Scripture again, followed by this reflection:

∽ What conversion of mind, heart, and life is the Lord asking of me?

_____

_____

_____

_____

∽ *Some Sadducees . . . came forward and put this question to Jesus.* Where do I go to find answers? What question would I ask Jesus?

_____

_____

_____

_____

≈ *Teacher, Moses wrote for us. . . .* Who have been my teachers in the faith? What role does Scripture play in my life of faith?

_____

_____

_____

_____

≈ *Those who are deemed worthy to attain to the coming age. . .* How am I preparing my heart and soul for the coming age? How can I grow in my fidelity to the Gospel?

_____

_____

_____

_____

≈ *After a period of silent reflection and/or discussion, all recite the Lord's Prayer and the following:*

Closing Prayer

Hear, O Lord, a just suit;
    attend to my outcry;
    hearken to my prayer from lips without deceit.

My steps have been steadfast in your paths,
    my feet have not faltered.
I call upon you, for you will answer me, O God;
    incline your ear to me; hear my word.

Keep me as the apple of your eye,
    hide me in the shadow of your wings.
But I in justice shall behold your face;
    on waking I shall be content in your presence.

From Psalm 17

Living the Word This Week

How can I make my life a gift for others in charity?

Research the catechetical efforts of your parish and prayerfully
consider how you might become involved.

November 13, 2022

Lectio Divina for the Thirty-Third Week in Ordinary Time

We begin our prayer:

In the name of the Father, and of the Son, and of the Holy Spirit. Amen.

Grant us, we pray, O Lord our God,
the constant gladness of being devoted to you,
for it is full and lasting happiness
to serve with constancy
the author of all that is good.
Through our Lord Jesus Christ, your Son,
who lives and reigns with you in the unity of the Holy Spirit,
God, for ever and ever.

Collect, Thirty-Third Sunday in Ordinary Time

Reading (*Lectio*)

Read the following Scripture two or three times.

Luke 21:5-19

While some people were speaking about how the temple was adorned with costly stones and votive offerings, Jesus said, "All that you see here—the days will come when there will not be left a stone upon another stone that will not be thrown down."

Then they asked him, "Teacher, when will this happen? And what sign will there be when all these things are about to happen?" He answered, "See that you not be deceived, for many will come in my name, saying, 'I am he,' and 'The time has come.' Do not follow them! When you hear of wars and insurrections, do not be terrified; for such things must happen first, but it will not immediately be the end." Then he said to them, "Nation will rise against nation, and kingdom against kingdom. There will be powerful earthquakes, famines, and plagues from place to place; and awesome sights and mighty signs will come from the sky.

"Before all this happens, however, they will seize and persecute you, they will hand you over to the synagogues and to prisons, and they will have you led before kings and governors because of my name. It will lead to your giving testimony. Remember, you are not to prepare your defense beforehand, for I myself shall give you a wisdom in speaking that all your adversaries will be powerless to resist or refute. You will even be handed over by parents, brothers, relatives, and friends, and they will put some of you to death. You will be hated by all because of my name, but not a hair on your head will be destroyed. By your perseverance you will secure your lives."

Meditation (*Meditatio*)

After the reading, take some time to reflect in silence on one or more of the following questions:

- What word or words in this passage caught your attention?
- What in this passage comforted you?
- What in this passage challenged you?

If practicing lectio divina as a family or in a group, after the reflection time, invite the participants to share their responses.

Prayer (*Oratio*)

Read the scripture passage one more time. Bring to the Lord the praise, petition, or thanksgiving that the Word inspires in you.

Contemplation (*Contemplatio*)

Read the Scripture again, followed by this reflection:

≈ What conversion of mind, heart, and life is the Lord asking of me?

_____

_____

_____

_____

~ Some people were speaking about how the temple was adorned with costly stones and votive offerings. How does the beauty of my parish church foster my worship of God? When has religious art nurtured my faith?

_____

_____

_____

_____

~ They will seize and persecute you. When have I suffered for my faith? How can I support those who are persecuted for their faith?

_____

_____

_____

_____

~ It will lead to your giving testimony. How have I given testimony to my faith this week? In the week ahead, how can I share my faith with words and actions?

_____

_____

_____

_____

≈ After a period of silent reflection and/or discussion, all recite the Lord's Prayer and the following:

Closing Prayer

Sing praise to the LORD with the harp,
  with the harp and melodious song.
With trumpets and the sound of the horn
  sing joyfully before the King, the LORD.

Let the sea and what fills it resound,
  the world and those who dwell in it;
let the rivers clap their hands,
  the mountains shout with them for joy.

Before the LORD, for he comes,
  for he comes to rule the earth,
He will rule the world with justice
  and the peoples with equity.

From Psalm 98

Living the Word This Week

How can I make my life a gift for others in charity?

Learn more about religious freedom and religious persecution around the world: *www.usccb.org/committees/religious-liberty/backgrounder -religious-freedom*.

November 20, 2022

Lectio Divina for the Solemnity of Our Lord Jesus Christ, King of the Universe

We begin our prayer:

In the name of the Father, and of the Son, and of the Holy Spirit. Amen.

Almighty ever-living God,
whose will is to restore all things
in your beloved Son, the King of the universe,
grant, we pray,
that the whole creation, set free from slavery,
may render your majesty service
and ceaselessly proclaim your praise.
Through our Lord Jesus Christ, your Son,
who lives and reigns with you in the unity of the Holy Spirit,
God, for ever and ever.

Collect, Solemnity of Our Lord Jesus Christ, King of the Universe

Reading (*Lectio*)

Read the following Scripture two or three times.

Luke 23:35-43

> The rulers sneered at Jesus and said, "He saved others, let him save himself if he is the chosen one, the Christ of God." Even the soldiers jeered at him. As they approached to offer him wine they called out, "If you are King of the Jews, save yourself." Above him there was an inscription that read, "This is the King of the Jews."

> Now one of the criminals hanging there reviled Jesus, saying, "Are you not the Christ? Save yourself and us." The other, however, rebuking him, said in reply, "Have you no fear of God, for you are subject to the same condemnation? And indeed, we have been condemned justly, for the sentence we received corresponds to our crimes, but this man has done nothing criminal." Then he said, "Jesus, remember me when you come into your kingdom." He replied to him, "Amen, I say to you, today you will be with me in Paradise."

Meditation (*Meditatio*)

After the reading, take some time to reflect in silence on one or more of the following questions:

- What word or words in this passage caught your attention?
- What in this passage comforted you?
- What in this passage challenged you?

If practicing lectio divina as a family or in a group, after the reflection time, invite the participants to share their responses.

Prayer (*Oratio*)

Read the scripture passage one more time. Bring to the Lord the praise, petition, or thanksgiving that the Word inspires in you.

Contemplation (*Contemplatio*)

Read the Scripture again, followed by this reflection:

~ What conversion of mind, heart, and life is the Lord asking of me?

_____

_____

_____

_____

~ *The rulers sneered at Jesus. . . . Even the soldiers jeered at him.* When I have judged or ridiculed others for their faith? When have I been judged or ridiculed?

_____

_____

_____

_____

≈ *We have been condemned justly.* What sinful behaviors do I need to turn away from? How can I seek God's grace and mercy to help my ongoing conversion?

_____

_____

_____

_____

≈ *Amen, I say to you, today you will be with me in Paradise.* What grounds my hope? How can I bring hope to my environment?

_____

_____

_____

_____

≈ *After a period of silent reflection and/or discussion, all recite the Lord's Prayer and the following:*

Closing Prayer

I rejoiced because they said to me,
    "We will go up to the house of the Lord."
And now we have set foot
    within your gates, O Jerusalem.

Jerusalem, built as a city
    with compact unity.
To it the tribes go up,
    the tribes of the LORD.

According to the decree for Israel,
    to give thanks to the name of the LORD.
In it are set up judgment seats,
    seats for the house of David.

From Psalm 122

Living the Word This Week

How can I make my life a gift for others in charity?

Read about prayer as a school of hope in paragraphs 32-34 of *Spe Salvi*: *www.vatican.va/content/benedict-xvi/en/encyclicals/documents/hf_ben-xvi_enc_20071130_spe-salvi.html.*